Joseph

Bound

Under

The

Guile

Of the

Devil

By Erica Boerman

Don't miss out on the experience!

Access your FREE Study Guide TODAY!

http://visitor.r20.constantcontact.com/d.jsp?llr=qyarwexab&p=oi&m
=1124365533968&sit=z7tlokqkb&f=8298aefb-3e02-419e-b440-
610589fe255a

This book is dedicated to two people influential people in my life

1) My mother, Norma Bither who taught me how to study God's Word. Every day I would see you and dad with your Bibles at the dining room table, you with your cup of Constant Comment Tea. You provided such a safe, loving, home that permeated with godliness. I learned the importance of persistence in daily devotionals. I learned to love God's Word and to search for its meaning like diving for treasure. I am eternally grateful!

2) My biological mother, Joni Stanchfield. So many times I saw you in the life of Joseph. Your determination to push past the pain and embrace what God has for your future is truly inspiring. I can't wait to see what God has in store for you and I count it a privilege to be able to walk this road with you!

I would not be where I am today without these women.

But God...

Joseph's life can be summed up in one phrase from Genesis 50:20 "…but God intended it for good to accomplish what is now being done, the saving of many lives." Whatever happened to him in his life (almost enough to make me buckle under the sheer thought of the opposition), God had a bigger plan and purpose which was the saving of many lives. Joseph had every reason to be bitter, resentful, defeated, and depressed; and I'm sure he experienced those feelings many times along the journey. However, through the trials, he set his mind on God and His purposes. Joseph was born into an impossible situation: He was a despised sibling who deserved some jealous reactions, but not the death that his brothers wanted to give him. He was a slave, prisoner, and ruler. God used those circumstances to change an afraid, arrogant, self-righteous tattletale into one who was in charge of saving not just many lives, but entire nations.

Whatever Satan has planned for you and whatever oppositions, struggles or even just the day to day monotony of laundry and meal planning, God's ultimate purpose is the saving of many lives. You may not ever see the fruit this side of Glory, but you can bet that God is working a master plan! Where your mind goes – down the rabbit hole of anxiety, defeat, "overwhelmedness" or fixed, albeit sometimes by sheer grit, on the cross will ultimately determine how you fare on the other side of trials. Will you wallow in self-pity? Will you blame others? Will you despair and retreat inward? Will you manipulate to get your way? Will you put on a façade and fake your way through life? That is what Satan wants more than anything. He wants your focus off of God. Therefore, your answer, *my* answer to everything that he throws at us must always, unquestioningly be "BUT GOD." The first words out of your mouth when you are feeling like a failure, a fraud or a freak should be, "BUT GOD."

But God says in His word that His word will not return void so I can pray His scripture over this situation because His word is truth and can be trusted.

But God says I am fearfully and wonderfully made so I will choose to see myself as He sees me: beautiful, a prized possession, His child.

But God says that children are an inheritance from the Lord, so I am in the exact moment at the perfect time to raise these blessings he has given me – *He* chose *me* to be *their* mom.

But God says that love covers a multitude of sins and because he has forgiven me, by His leading, I can forgive_____.

But God says that He is with me always, even to the very end, so I do not have to be afraid of the medical tests coming up.

But God says that He has removed our sins as far from us as the east is from the west so I can leave my past in the past. It is finished. Christ has died and covered my sins in His righteousness.

But God says that to be absent from the body is to be present with the Lord, so I know I will see my parent, spouse, child, sibling, friend, loved one again.

But God says that he will *never* leave me or forsake me, so I will put my hope and trust in a God who loves and cares for me deeply even if I don't feel His presence right now. It doesn't mean that He's not here.

When we turn from the rabbit hole to the truth found in God's word and take every thought captive, we will be able to see our circumstances from His perspective and like Joseph, we'll be able to say, "But God intends this for good."

We will then be able to see a glimpse of who God is. We will be able to, "[u]nderstand, therefore, that the LORD [our] God is indeed God. He is the faithful God who keeps his covenant for a thousand generations and lavishes his unfailing love on those who love him and obey his commands (Deuteronomy 7:9 NLT)." He is faithful. He will keep His promises to my parents, to me, to my children and to my grandchildren and beyond! *That* is a God who has it all under His control and can be trusted in the nitty gritty, day to day stuff of life as well as the hardships, trauma, and crippling circumstances.

Chapter 1
Idolizing Your Child

Satan wants you to be more concerned about the performance, appearance and behavior of your child than about the child's character.
BUT GOD wants you to be satisfied and content with life as it is because when your home is child-centric, there is less of a focus on the discipling of your child, which is essential in bringing up the next generation of Christ followers.

Genesis 30:22-24

Then God remembered Rachel; he listened to her and opened her womb. She became pregnant and gave birth to a son and said, 'God has taken away my disgrace.' She named him Joseph and said, "May the LORD add to me another son (NIV)."

Before Joseph even had a chance to make a name for himself or learn to play with his father's multi-patterned sheep or even to stay away from the adder, he had a destiny placed upon his head. He would be known as Jacob's favorite son. He was also his mother's firstborn after a long time of infertility. Talk about pressure! In ONE moment – at the cries of a newborn, a whole clan was changed. Even his name, which essentially meant dissatisfaction, had connotations of pressure. His mother named him Joseph and said, "May the LORD add to me another son (Genesis 30:24 NIV)."

Like Jacob and Rachel, there are many parents who idolize their children. They set them up on unnecessary pedestals. In Ted Cunningham's book, Trophy Child, he says, "Children have become an extension of their parents. Mom and Dad exhaust themselves with the performance of their children. They offer constant praise in an attempt to build self-esteem. We have placed our children in the driver's seat (26-27)." He says that parents in the 1980's "began shifting their style to be more encouraging, nurturing, and praising, bombarding kids with excessive 'atta-boys,' gold stars for every paper, no-loser competitions, no-failure-allowed assignments, big moments on the stage or field, and plenty of opportunity and privilege... Parents misinterpret love. They believe they are doing their children a service by elevating them and overencouraging them. They believe this is the best way to communicate love, not realizing the damage caused by revolving the world around their children (22-23)."

The devil wants us to be so concerned with performance and so busy with our children's activities that we do not have time or energy to serve God. We no longer make carved images for our idols today, but our idols can be our own flesh and blood. We can look to our children for satisfaction, companionship or status as a good mom. It is ok to be proud of your child and to tell them often. You must be honest with yourself, though. Are you proud because they achieve more or behave better than other children on the block? Or are you proud because God has given your child real talents and is developing those gifts in him or her? If you search your soul, you will be able to tell when you have crossed the line into idolization.

You cannot live your life for your children's enhancement. By enrolling them in every sport or activity just because the world says that they have to start participating early to succeed is utter lunacy. Sports, dance, music and educational clubs are not awful ideas, but when we do it because deep down it makes us feel good to have an overachiever, or junior following in our footsteps, it will absorb our focus and energy. The focus lifts off the character development and "disciple-making" of the child, and moves to performance, appearance and competing with other families.

When we revolve our lives around our children and do not allow for date nights with our spouses, or our own spiritual and personal betterment, we are idolizing our child and their abilities. We must not negatively push them to succeed and miss the precious presence of the child himself. When too much pressure is placed on the child, your focus remains earthly instead of eternal.

No child ever looks back and says, "Remember when I got carted around and we rushed here and there and ate McDonald's three nights out of the week? That was so great!! I'm glad we never sat down to a family meal and talked about our day and hashed out friendships and dating relationships and the hard things of life. I'm so glad we were so busy that we avoided all depth. Thank you, Mom and Dad!" If you are running around like a chicken with your head cut off, disguising it as bettering your child and hoping that it is giving them a childhood, you are fooling yourself.

A childhood should be spent catching fireflies and eating a meal together as a family. It is cuddling on the couch to watch a special movie because they *don't* watch television all afternoon long! It's taking hikes in the forest or swimming in the ocean as a family. We have our children for such a small amount of time. Why would we want to spend that time away from the house or family? They are only with us for a quarter of their lives and Heaven help us all because six of those years, they're teenagers! Do you really want to spend it away from your home and away from each other? Why bother even having children? You don't want a child; you want a trophy. Don't be like Rachel. Don't look for something better or something more. Look at the very child in front of you and be pleased with them alone. Be pleased with who God created him or her to be and the fact you get to parent that child! What a blessing! You are in the exact season of life you are supposed to be in. Embrace it. Revel in it. Love it. *Thrive* in it!

SATAN WANTS YOU TO LIFT YOUR CHILD ONTO A PEDESTAL AND OBTAIN FULFILLMENT FROM HIS/HER ACCOMPLISHMENTS IN SCHOOL OR EXTRACURRICULAR ACTIVITIES. HE WANTS YOU TO REVOLVE YOUR LIFE AROUND YOUR CHILD: OVER ENCOURAGING, INDULGING AND REMAINING BUSY CARTING CHILDREN HERE AND THERE. HE DOES NOT WANT YOU SPENDING QUALITY TIME TOGETHER AS AN INTACT FAMILY UNIT BECAUSE HE KNOWS IF A FAMILY IS STRONG, IT CAN CHANGE THE COMMUNITY, STATE, COUNTRY AND THEN THE WORLD! SATAN WANTS YOU TO MAKE AN IDOL OUT OF YOUR CHILD, AND DISGUISES IT, WRAPPED UP IN A PRETTY BOW, CALLING IT LOVE.

BUT GOD WANTS YOU TO ACKNOWLEDGE YOUR CHILD AS A BLESSING. HE WANTS YOU TO BE CONTENT WITH WHAT HE HAS GIVEN YOU. HE WANTS YOU TO THRIVE WHERE HE HAS PUT YOU AND WITH THE PEOPLE HE HAS PLACED IN YOUR HOME. IF YOUR CHILD SPENDS MORE TIME WITH OTHER PEOPLE THAN WITH YOU BECAUSE THEY ARE IN AN ENDLESS AMOUNT OF ACTIVITIES, YOU ARE NOT DOING THE JOB GOD CALLED YOU TO DO. IF YOU ARE CONSTANTLY PUSHING YOUR CHILD TOWARD EXCELLENCE BECAUSE YOU NEED PERFECTION (SOMETHING I AM QUITE GUILTY OF) THEN YOU ARE NOT DOING YOUR JOB AS THE PARENT GOD CREATED YOU TO BE. GOD WANTS YOU TO PRIORITIZE RIGHTLY, SET UP REASONABLE EXPECTATIONS AND NOT BE SO DRIVEN TOWARD WORLDLY SUCCESS VIA YOUR CHILDREN. YOU ARE RAISING THE NEXT GENERATION OF CHRISTIANS AND HE WANTS YOU TO RAISE THEM TO BE HOLY; NOT BE TOO BUSY AND CONCENTRATED ON YOUR CHILD OR YOUR CHILD'S PERFORMANCE.

Chapter 2

Faith Testimonies

Satan wants you to live in fear instead of remembering how God has been faithful and true in the past.
BUT GOD wants you to acknowledge in your heart and proclaim with your lips your unique faith testimony that promotes the idea that God was with you wherever you went and no matter what you faced; He never left you and fulfilled all of His promises to you.

Genesis 31:19-23, 26-37; 32:6-8

When Laban had gone to shear his sheep, Rachel stole her father's household gods. Moreover, Jacob deceived Laban the Aramean by not telling him he was running away. So he fled with all he had, crossed the Euphrates River, and headed for the hill country of Gilead.

On the third day Laban was told that Jacob had fled. Taking his relatives with him, he pursued Jacob for seven days and caught up with him in the hill country of Gilead...Then Laban said to Jacob, "What have you done? You've deceived me, and you've carried off my daughters like captives in war. Why did you run off secretly and deceive me? Why didn't you tell me, so I could send you away with joy and singing to the music of timbrels and harps? You didn't even let me kiss my grandchildren and my daughters goodbye. You have done a foolish thing. I have the power to harm you; but last night the God of your father said to me, 'Be careful not to say anything to Jacob, either good or bad.' Now you have gone off because you longed to return to your father's household. But why did you steal my gods?"

Jacob answered Laban, "I was afraid, because I thought you would take your daughters away from me by force. But if you find anyone who has your gods, that person shall not live. In the presence of our relatives, see for yourself whether there is anything of yours here with me; and if so, take it." Now Jacob did not know that Rachel had stolen the gods. So Laban went into Jacob's tent and into Leah's tent and into the tent of the two female servants, but he found nothing. After he came out of Leah's tent, he entered Rachel's tent. Now Rachel had taken the household gods and put them inside her camel's saddle and was sitting on them. Laban searched through everything in the tent but found nothing. Rachel said to her father, "Don't be angry, my lord, that I cannot stand up in your presence; I'm having my period." So he searched but could not find the household gods.

Jacob was angry and took Laban to task. "What is my crime?" he asked Laban. "How have I wronged you that you hunt me down? Now that you have searched through all my goods, what have you found that belongs to your household? Put it here in front of your relatives and mine, and let them judge between the two of us...[As Jacob set out after a truce between him and his in-laws, he sent messengers to bring greetings to his brother Esau.]

When the messengers returned to Jacob, they said, "We went to your brother Esau, and now he is coming to meet you, and four hundred men are with him." In great fear and distress Jacob divided the people who were with him into two groups, and the flocks and herds and camels as well. He thought, "If Esau comes and attacks one group, the group that is left may escape (NIV)."

Within about ten years since Joseph's birth, He and his family will have left his manipulative grandfather, only to be hunted and tracked down by him and his men. What a fright that must have been for a child. I remember a time when I was about 6 years old and my parents needed me to go to a babysitter after Vacation Bible School one day. I went to a boy's house that afternoon. I have only been there once, but this event had such an impact on me, I won't ever forget the way it looked. There was a decent amount of land, though it wasn't pretty. It was city land – a double lot. The house was a two story with white aluminum siding. I believe it might have been a duplex and this little boy lived with his aunt and grandmother on the upper level. We walked into the kitchen. The sink was to the left and the table was to the right against the wall. The aunt's bedroom was directly in back of that.

It was about 3 o'clock and we were playing out in the back yard when his grandmother yelled for us to come inside. There was fear in her voice, and we had to run up the wooden stairs as fast as we could. As we did, a white car came into the backyard. A skinny man dressed in jeans and a white T-shirt with the sleeves cut off got out of the car. He was yelling and screaming but I couldn't make out what he was saying. We were yanked inside by the aunt and whisked into her room. We had to be totally silent while the grandmother dealt with this man. We took turns leaning over and looking out of the key hole in her room.

The grandmother remained calm and spoke gently to this man who was obviously mad about something. He began slamming his hand down on the table and I couldn't figure out what they were fighting about. Then it became clear. He was this boy's father and wanted the boy to go with him, but he was intoxicated, so the grandmother wasn't going to allow it. He became irate, and the grandmother threatened to call the police. He became irate so the grandmother threatened to call the police. That scared him off, but not before he took out his anger on his car and the nearby garbage cans before peeling out of the driveway and down the road. I was crying, wanting nothing by my dad to come and get me. I didn't feel safe until he came a little while later. It's been thirty years and I can still remember my terror that day.

Can you imagine what these children felt as they secretly stole away from their grandfather's house, only to be tracked down? I'm sure there was tension in the camp. In front of everyone, Joseph witnessed his grandfather accuse his father of being a thief and then proceed to ransack the whole camp. When he had finished his tirade, Joseph's father then lit into his grandfather, accusing him of being a liar and a manipulative cheat! Finally, the two men settled down and came to an agreement. *All the while*, Joseph's mother had *indeed* stolen what his grandfather was searching for and then sat on the stolen idols and lied about having her period. I would be willing to bet that as the favored child, he might have had an idea that his mother had stolen the gods.

As if that stressful encounter is not enough: a little while later, Jacob hears that his brother Esau is coming out to meet him with an army! This situation gets even more tense when Joseph witnesses his father parting with all of his possessions in order to hopefully pacify his uncle, whom he has never met. I am sure Joseph knew the history of the two brothers: Jacob had run away from Esau when he threatened to kill him! Family drama doesn't get much worse than that! Just when Joseph thought it was safe, he's now forced to meet a man face to face that wanted to kill his father. No one knew it was going to end so peacefully.

Can you imagine this little boy's terror? His father made it clear that all those going before them could be slaughtered. Then the realization must have kicked in, "I could be slaughtered!" What a nightmare! All around his tenth year of life! When I compare it to my frightening memory as a six-year-old that lasted only about an hour, I can only imagine how much greater his terror must have been and how it affected him in the years to come.

Another event Joseph might have remembered that probably helped him while in bondage in Egypt was something that happened just a short time after leaving Esau. Around this same time, his half-sister Dinah was raped by a leading official in the next town over. His half-brothers convinced the whole town to circumcise themselves in order to allow this one prominent figure to marry Dinah. While all of the men of the village were "recuperating," Levi and Simeon attacked the town, killed all of the men and took away plunder including all of the women and children (Genesis 34 NIV). After this, God told Jacob to high tail it out of there for Bethel. Jacob obeyed as the text says, "So Jacob said to his household and to all who were with him, "Get rid of the foreign gods you have with you, and purify yourselves and change your clothes. Then come, let us go up to Bethel, where I will build an altar to God, who answered me in the day of my distress and who has been with me wherever I have gone (Genesis 35:2-3 NIV)."

Jacob told everyone in his household, which included all the new women and children from the town that was ransacked, to purify themselves and to get rid of anything that would remind them of a god other than the True God. He says that he plans to build an altar to God "who answered [him] in the day of [his] distress and who has been with [him] wherever [he has] gone (Genesis 35:3 NIV)." This faith testimony must have had a big impact on Joseph because he had just witnessed three scary situations and God's deliverance three times as well. With all the tumult and stress, what was said by his father would have been cemented in his mind. Just like everything about the house I went to when I was six is cemented in my mind, I bet this faith testimony held great weight and permanence. This statement about God's unfailing help and continual presence in time of distress not only reverberated between Joseph's ears as a child but also during captivity. If his father could recognize that God was with him wherever he went, no matter the town, country or enemy, Joseph could remember that God was also with himself in Egypt.

Our children are listening. They hear the distress in our voices. They know when there is tension in the house. They may not know that dad walked out or lost his job, but they know something is causing an undercurrent of anxiety. Even babies sense when mom is upset. They will cry, stop nursing and generally fuss if mom is worried, anxious, crying or frustrated. Our children are smarter than we give them credit for. They understand when all is not right in the climate at home and will often act out to try to balance the crazy that they feel inside. How we handle crises will have a direct effect on our children's faith. Will our "faith testimonies" convey that we serve a trustworthy God? Or will they convey that we have to solve our problems on our own in a cruel and uncertain world?

It is our job in these moments to be vulnerable with our children. I think that is what Jacob does. He tells them that he is going to "build an altar to God" in the exact place where "God revealed himself to [Jacob] when he fled from his brother (Genesis 35:3b, 7 NIV)." Surely Jacob told his family what had transpired the first time he was in Bethel. God had shown him a vision as he was fleeing his murderous brother, Esau. The vision was of a staircase reaching from Heaven to Earth with angels going up and down. God stood at the top and said, "I am with you and will watch over you wherever you go, and I will bring you back to this land. I will not leave you until I have done what I have promised you (Genesis 28:15 NIV)." His whole purpose in building that altar there in that moment was to remember "God, who answered [him] in the day of [his] distress and who has been with [him] wherever [he has] gone (NIV)." Much had transpired since he traveled through Bethel on his way to his uncle's house to ask if he could find someone within the family to marry. Jacob had come a long way and is remembering God's goodness, protection and provision. Do your children know this? Do they know that God is with you wherever you go and whatever you face? Have you told them of His faithfulness, deliverance and guidance?

When we are facing times of uncertainty and fear, what do our children see us doing? Do they see us wringing our hands and worrying nonstop or do they see us in prayer seeking God? If we can take a breath long enough to acknowledge God's faithfulness in the past, we can lower the tension in the home enough to demonstrate to our family that God is with us wherever we go and in whatever circumstances we face both presently and in the future. We need to be examples to our children of how to respond constructively to whatever life throws at us. By acknowledging our sin or our vulnerability, our children can see God working through our weakness. His strength will be elevated!

What are your children picking up on in your home? Is it peaceful or is there tension? Whatever is happening, are you communicating faith in who God is and His deep connection and concern with the lives of all His children? Are you giving little testimonies of faith out loud to your children in those teachable moments? Are you acknowledging your mistakes, being vulnerable with your children and showing them how God has kept His promises? This is not as easy as it seems. I don't do enough of it myself. It requires conscious effort.

One of the best ways to slip in some "faith testimonies" are to have family dinners together. The dinner table should be a safe place. Some of our favorite conversations happen around the table. This is something I learned in childhood. The family dinner table had such an impact on me that when my parents asked me what piece of furniture I wanted when they passed away I did not even think about it, "The table!" I exclaimed. We, as parents, can communicate who God is and what He is accomplishing and how we've seen Him working that day. It is humbling to witness this sense of safe community being passed on to my children. As an example, during one dinnertime conversation in which my husband and I were expressing some serious concerns over the direction our children's school was taking, my daughter piped up, "I just love how you two talk about things! This is so great!" It made her feel secure and safe to watch Mom and Dad discuss a difficult situation and to try to see God's hand at work.

Focus on the Family President, Jim Daly in his article, "Nourish Your Family....As a Family" asks us to consider the following:

- The largest federally funded study of American teenagers found a strong link between regular family meals and academic success. Eating dinner together also led to improved psychological health, as well as lower rates of alcohol and drug abuse, early sexual activity and suicide.
- A 2005 Columbia University study found that teenagers who eat with their families at least five times a week are more likely to get better grades and less likely to have substance abuse problems. In fact, the University of Michigan found that a regular family mealtime is the single greatest predictor of improved achievement — more than studying, sports or other school activities.
- A study of preschoolers found that mealtime conversations with children helped to build vocabulary more effectively than listening to stories or even reading aloud.
- Eating together as a family also appears to decrease the likelihood of teenagers developing eating disorders. Research conducted in Minnesota found that adolescent girls who ate with their families at least five times a week were at far less risk for anorexia and bulimia than girls who didn't eat with their families."

Eating together and having safe community around the table with your loved ones is essential to development both physically and emotionally. Being able to recount how God has been faithful and trustworthy will help your children as they grow and leave the home.

You might also consider having a bedtime routine that includes spending a few minutes with your children so you can talk about anything that is on their minds. Kids are often happy to have meaningful conversations at bedtime because they don't want to go to sleep. They'll talk your ear off! It is worth it to start going to bed a little earlier so that you can capitalize on those precious moments of connection. Our family tries to ask, "What was one thing about today that you were grateful for? What is something that you need encouragement for?" When our children are experiencing something that we have been through before, we are able to recall those stories and testify to how God delivered us, disciplined us or increased our faith. Our children can see how God was faithful to us when we were young and how He continues to be faithful even now! It is vitally important to your children's faith to see you be vulnerable and pull your strength from God. We do not want them to grow up believing the myth that we have it all together and therefore do not need God. If we do not show them our vulnerability and ultimate reliance on God, our children may conclude that Jesus is more of an accessory than a Savior.

SATAN DOES NOT WANT YOU TO TAKE THE TIME TO SHOW YOUR CHILDREN GOD'S FAITHFULNESS. HE WANTS YOU TO FORGET ABOUT WHAT GOD HAS DONE FOR YOU IN THE PAST. HE WANTS YOU TO FORGET HOW GOD HAS LED YOU. HE WANTS YOU TO FORGET GOD'S PROVISION. HE CERTAINLY DOES NOT WANT YOU TO CONVEY GOD'S KEPT PROMISES TO YOUR CHILDREN. HE WANTS YOU TO LIVE IN FEAR, DESPAIR, REJECTION AND SELF-RELIANCE.

BUT GOD WANTS YOU TO REMEMBER AND BELIEVE! HE WANTS YOU TO ACKNOWLEDGE HIS GUIDANCE AND PRESENCE TO THE NEXT GENERATION BY EXPRESSING YOUR "FAITH TESTIMONIES." DURING TIMES OF FEAR AND UNCERTAINTY, GOD WANTS US TO RECALL HIS FAITHFULNESS OVER THE YEARS BY LOOKING

AT OUR PAST, SEEING HIS TRUSTWORTHINESS AND THEN PROCLAIMING IT. THEN WE CAN GET RID OF SELF-RELIANCE AND DEPEND ON THE ONE WHO *NEVER* LEAVES US UNTIL HE HAS DONE WHAT HE HAS PROMISED!

STOP! BEFORE YOU GO ANY FURTHER, ACCESS THE **FREE, DOWNLOADABLE** *Study Guide* HERE:

http://visitor.r20.constantcontact.com/d.jsp?llr=qyarwexab&p=oi&m=1124365533968&sit=z7tlokqkb&f=8298aefb-3e02-419e-b440-610589fe255a

Chapter 3
Who's Toxic: You or The Other Person?

Satan does not want you to take any responsibility for sour relationships; he also does not want you to recognize when the better option would be to leave a toxic relationship.
BUT GOD wants you to thrive and grow in your relationships giving you wisdom to see where the fault lies: with you, or with the other person. Once you can understand who needs to take responsibility, you can act accordingly either repenting and turning away from your own sin; or distancing yourself from that toxic relationship.

Genesis 37:2b-11

Joseph, a young man of seventeen, was tending the flocks with his brothers, the sons of Bilhah and the sons of Zilpah, his father's wives, and he brought their father a bad report about them. Now Israel loved Joseph more than any of his other sons, because he had been born to him in his old age; and he made an ornate robe for him. When his brothers saw that their father loved him more than any of them, they hated him and could not speak a kind word to him. Joseph had a dream, and when he told it to his brothers, they hated him all the more. He said to them, "Listen to this dream I had: We were binding sheaves of grain out in the field when suddenly my sheaf rose and stood upright, while your sheaves gathered around mine and bowed down to it." His brothers said to him, "Do you intend to reign over us? Will you actually rule us?" And they hated him all the more because of his dream and what he had said. Then he had another dream, and he told it to his brothers. "Listen," he said, "I had another dream, and this time the sun and moon and eleven stars were bowing down to me." When he told his father as well as his brothers, his father rebuked him and said, "What is this dream you had? Will your mother and I and your brothers actually come and bow down to

the ground before you?" His brothers were jealous of him, but his father kept the matter in mind (NIV).

Seven years after the turbulent departure from his birthplace and the confrontation between his father and his uncle, Joseph grew into a young man who, like most seventeen year olds, was overly confident in his knowledge and stature. Joseph's brothers saw him for who they thought he was: an arrogant tattle-tale, favored above all of them. He was used to getting his own way. He was the father's favorite and they hated him because of it. Look closely, the passage mentions the hatred of Joseph's brothers for him three times.

Maybe your siblings resent you because they think you were the favorite. Or Maybe you weren't the favorite. Maybe you were the one always in trouble, the black sheep. You've never fit in. You say the wrong things, do everything backwards, are always late and disappoint them at every turn. You try harder to engage them and try to relate to them but they are so full of disdain for you that even that seems to ignite anger within them. So you give them space and you're accused of shunning the family. What can you do? You're not sure you know what you did in the first place to incite such animosity.

It is completely possible that you did something to warrant this behavior from your family. Maybe you rebelled in your youth and committed acts that they haven't forgiven you for yet. Maybe you've never grown up. They are confused and cannot treat you like the adolescent you still act like because you are much older, but also can't treat you like the adult you are because of your irresponsible behavior. Maybe, though, they are just toxic people in your life.

Take an honest look at yourself first. Be willing to entertain the idea that you are mostly to blame.

- Is there something about your demeanor that causes others outside your family to chafe?
- What was the last disagreement you had with one of your friends?
- Were there any themes that came out that are similar, at least in part, to what your family has said to you in the past?

- Could you have committed an offense in your youth that you thought you had repented of and asked forgiveness for but they could still be angry about it?
- If you're married, when you have disagreements with your spouse, is there something that he says over and over again? Is there a complaint that is repeated – it never seems to go away?

Those are the questions you must ask as you humbly pray to God to reveal your part in the conflict. It is very possible that you must take responsibility for your actions in a way that is wrought with humility and true repentance. Nothing less than an acknowledgement of your shortcomings and taking full responsibility for your arrogance, misbehavior and lack of concern for others will suffice.

However, it is also equally possible that you are not to blame at all. Sometimes there are people in your life that are so broken and hurting that all they want to do is break and hurt others. They can feign niceties and reel you in, only to cut you loose on a whim. This happens over and over again.

When my grandmother passed away, my grandfather was distraught. It hurt my heart to see him so sad. I love my grandfather and would do anything for him. I am a do-er. That is how I cope with pain, I do something about it. His one concern was that he wanted people to go through his house and her possessions. After the funeral I had an extra day to spend with my grandfather before I had to return home. I asked my grandfather if there was anything that he needed done since I was there and I had a whole day to devote to helping him. My grandfather did not even know where he would want me to start, so my mother had suggested to him that I start going through my grandmother's clothes. When my father had passed away several years earlier, she said that emptying his closet was the one thing that really helped her the most because she wouldn't have been able to do it. My grandfather perked up at that suggestion and thought that that would be a really good idea.

I went over to his house and I asked him where he wanted everything. He just wanted it packed up as quickly as possible in garbage bags. When a family member found out that I had gone through my grandmother's clothes, she was livid. Instead of assuming that I was trying to do something nice and kind for my grandfather, she called me disrespectful and told me I had no right to go through my grandmother's clothes without her permission. She told me that she was beside herself with anger toward me and that things would never be the same between us again. I was so deeply hurt by what she said because I thought I was doing something really nice for my grandfather. I felt joy at being able to serve him. I was grateful at being able to help out the family in that small way. I had ministered to him and I had been able to tangibly show him how much I loved and cared for him. In turn, it was a big aid in helping me cope with my own grief.

My heart was also broken on a much deeper level. You see, being adopted, even if it is within family, a child struggles with identity. Was I a Bither (my adoptive parents' family) or was a I a Miller (my biological family)? I did not think that I still struggled with that concept until this confrontation. In an instant a piece of my self-worth away was taken away. This conversation essentially told me my standing in the family as a granddaughter was significantly less than I had imagined. The pain and the hurt are still very raw and very real. I still struggle with anger toward this woman for her insensitivity, callousness and hateful words. I also know I am called to forgive and it is my deep desire to do so.

I have come to realize, however, that forgiveness does not mean that you forget everything or that restoration is required. It is imprudent to forget certain wrongs committed. Proverbs 26:11 says, "As a dog returns to its vomit, so a fool repeats his foolishness (NLT)."

There is wisdom in not going back into a situation where you will remain looked down upon and your self-worth will crumble. Joseph could not have produced the fruit he did and still remain under his father's tent with the older brothers constantly hating him. He had to be removed and replanted somewhere else. When he was removed, albeit forcibly, he was able to learn the art of forgiveness. Sometimes a removal from the situation is necessary because the toxic vines are choking you, keeping you paralyzed in the past. You need to hack away at the vines so they do not strangle the life completely out of you.

Please hear me, this cutting off of a toxic relationship comes after you have taken FULL responsibility for your part in the deterioration of the relationship. Do not dare to presume that God will bless a severance of a relationship when you blame others for having natural reactions to your irresponsible misbehavior. This drastic step is saved for when you have genuinely lived out what the Bible says in Romans 12:17b,18 "Respect what is right in the sight of all men. If possible, so far as it depends on you, be at peace with all men (NASB)." If, it has become quite apparent that you have done exactly that and you still get beaten down emotionally and your heart is breaking at every encounter, then it might be time to cut the relationship off. If your immediate family is going to be affected by the toxicity, then it is time to reevaluate the necessity of that relationship.

Severing ties with family members is not something to take lightly. However, it is something to consider, especially if you have young children who could be scarred by the interplay between you and the other party. It does not have to be a huge, dramatic exit. It can merely be a stopping of initiation on your part. Stop subjecting yourself and your family to unnecessary and cruel manipulation and ridicule. You simply stop. There are no angry words or spiteful banter. You simply stop taking the first step and therefore stop being a punching bag.

Boundaries are healthy. God created them. He put boundaries on the seas, the mountains, the amount of rainfall or snow squalls. They stop when He says, "Stop." They start at His prompting. God has made you the steward of your own life and you have a responsibility to live it for Him. You are of zero help to the Kingdom of God when you are preoccupied with family drama.

God called you to live boldly for Him, but quite possibly, you might be so downtrodden that your courage is gone. God called you to be His hands and feet, but if you're too busy living in the past and fearing the future that you cannot be fully present and *be* those hands and feet. You are either replaying in your mind the last conversations over and over again, or you're anxious in anticipation over your future contact. If you are constantly biting your nails or your stomach is in knots and you have to take antacid pills just to attend Christmas, stop doing it! Christmas will happen regardless of if you're there or not. You not showing up will not affect Jesus' birth. The first year will be the hardest, but let me give you a tip: this year, instead of dreading Christmas "festivities" with toxic family members, and instead of giving gifts to your children and spouse, could you all agree to go away on a nice trip together over the holiday? This way you could start a new family tradition. One built on excitement, anticipation and joy. Perhaps a change is necessary for you to thrive and fully become the child of God you are called to be.

SATAN WANTS YOU TO VACILLATE BETWEEN TWO THOUGHTS WHEN DEALING WITH INTERPERSONAL CONFLICT. EITHER YOU ARE A MARTYR AND NO ONE UNDERSTANDS YOU AND EVERYONE IS AGAINST YOU, OR YOU ARE A VICTIM OF VICIOUS PEOPLE, BUT BECAUSE YOU FEEL SOME SORT OF OBLIGATION TO CONTINUE THE RELATIONSHIP YOU SET YOURSELF UP FOR TORTURE TIME AND AGAIN. HE WANTS YOU TO WALLOW IN BITTERNESS OVER BEING WRONGED. HE WANTS YOU TO THINK YOU ARE NOT TO BLAME IN ANYTHING. HE DOES NOT WANT YOU TO TAKE THE HARD PATH TOWARD FORGIVENESS. ON THE OTHER HAND, HE DOES NOT WANT YOU TO CUT OFF THOSE TOXIC RELATIONSHIPS. HE WANTS YOU TO KEEP SUBJECTING YOURSELF TO THE DISCOMFORT AND PAIN BROUGHT ABOUT BY THESE RELATIONSHIPS CITING FAMILIAL TIES AS SOMETHING OBLIGATORY NO MATTER THE COST.

BUT GOD WANTS YOU TO RECOGNIZE WHEN YOU ARE TO BLAME FOR THE DETERIORATION OF A RELATIONSHIP AND TO TAKE RESPONSIBILITY. THAT MEANS PURSUING SOME SORT OF HELP ON CHANGING YOUR BEHAVIOR PATTERNS. HOWEVER, HE ALSO WANTS YOU TO THRIVE AND GROW AND IF THE RIFT IS TRULY NOT YOUR FAULT, HE DOES NOT WANT YOU TO BE SUBJECTED TO TOXIC

RELATIONSHIPS. THOSE RELATIONSHIPS THAT ARE DETRIMENTAL TO YOUR HEALTH, BOTH PHYSICAL AND MENTAL AS WELL AS THE OVERALL HEALTH AND ATMOSPHERE OF YOUR HOME SHOULD BE SCRUTINIZED AND THEIR NECESSITY IN YOUR LIFE EVALUATED.

Chapter 4

Staying True to Your Calling

Satan wants you to question God's calling on your life and will use any means necessary to insert doubt into your mind and heart. He will use your feelings, circumstances and others to try to derail you.
BUT GOD wants you to stay the course and remember that since He does not make a mistake, calling you to His purpose was therefore not a mistake; He will bring it to full completion and is faithful to stick with you to the very end.

Genesis 37:23-28

So when Joseph came to his brothers, they stripped him of his robe—the ornate robe he was wearing—and they took him and threw him into the cistern. The cistern was empty; there was no water in it. As they sat down to eat their meal, they looked up and saw a caravan of Ishmaelites coming from Gilead. Their camels were loaded with spices, balm and myrrh, and they were on their way to take them down to Egypt. Judah said to his brothers, "What will we gain if we kill our brother and cover up his blood? Come, let's sell him to the Ishmaelites and not lay our hands on him; after all, he is our brother, our own flesh and blood." His brothers agreed. So when the Midianite merchants came by, his brothers pulled Joseph up out of the cistern and sold him for twenty shekels of silver to the Ishmaelites, who took him to Egypt (NIV).

Getting thrown into a cistern was hardly better than being killed outright. "In the earliest times of the Bible cisterns were used to store water. They were usually pear shaped, and 15 to 20 feet deep, and the actual opening was only 2 to 3 feet. There was usually a stone cover. Cisterns were either large or small, large enough to store water for the community, or small and privately owned. Cisterns were like wells of water, which could be hoisted up with ropes and a bucket **(http://www.bible-history.com/biblestudy/cisterns.html)**." Fifteen feet is a significant height from which to fall. I often wonder what was going through Joseph's mind during his time in the cistern. Did he hear his brothers discussing ways to kill him? Did he hear them negotiating his sale? Did he pray?

I am assuming that he had at least considered his dreams and wondered where God was. God had called him. He knew it. He had two dreams that demonstrated that God was going to work great and mighty things. When something is repeated in the Bible it usually means there is something significant that requires a pause and a second look. There is a special emphasis and a point God is trying to make clear. In the first dream, the sheaves of grain from Joseph's brothers bowed down to Joseph's grain. As if that was not clear enough, in the second dream, the sun, moon and stars actually bowed down to Joseph the person – not just to his sheaves of grain. The sun, moon and stars are all throughout Scripture and are used in to indicate glory (Revelation12:1), something of great importance (Genesis 15:5), revelation (Psalm 19:1-4) and change (Genesis 1:14-15) to name a few (NIV).

Something significant was going to happen in the life of Joseph. He was going to be a leader, someone important. Even Jacob pondered this dream. Jacob had experienced the God of his salvation in a dream when he saw angels descending and ascending between heaven and earth. He knew the weight and value of something when the Almighty speaks in a dream. Being a favored son of the patriarch would give Joseph more insight into his father's inner thoughts. It is not a stretch of the imagination to think that when Joseph had those dreams, he was convinced that God had spoken directly to him.

Have you ever felt that way? God had called you to a bigger purpose than what you were living? You know God has something more. It may be a career change. It may be a volunteer opportunity. It may even be reclaiming what the enemy has conquered in your family. Perhaps you are going to buckle down and get serious about your faith and the trajectory of your life. A deep longing and enthusiasm fills your body. You are excited and expectant for God to work. He has given you an assurance and an excitement to see what He will do.

And then there is a road block. Something comes along to take the wind out of your sails. You no longer feel the excitement. Doubt creeps in. The Enemy of our souls whispers, "Did God really say? Are you sure you are called to do this? It doesn't appear as if people are responding favorably. You messed up. People are irritated, befuddled, and laughing at you. Is this worth it? You should just give up now and cut your losses." This is a dark, confusing place. It is an uncomfortable existence when you start doubting God's call. You wake up one day and say, "What am I doing? Who do I think I am? I am such a fool." I would assume Joseph felt this same way as his brothers stuffed him through a three-foot hole and he landed with a thud against the cold, dark ground. Who knows what kind of scorpions, spiders and snakes were in there.

Did Joseph think he would stay there forever and rot?

Did he think his brothers would try to shoot him with an arrow?

Did he wonder where God was?

Did he wonder if God had forgotten him?

What about his dream? Wasn't he destined for greatness?

Wasn't he supposed to be a prince?

Did God really say? Is God trustworthy? It took about thirteen years for Joseph's dreams to come true. He must have questioned God's sovereignty and God omniscience. Did God really say?

When you are faced with moments of uncertainty and you are faced with moments where you just don't know if you heard God correctly where can you turn? God wants for His children to draw near to Him. James 4:8a says, "Come close to God, and God will come close to you (NLT)." When you know that you've heard God speak to you, start your active obedience right then and there. Memorialize it somehow. When you memorialize this you will be able to look back on it during times of uncertainty. Countless times in the Old Testament God had the Israelites remember what He had done for them in Egypt. Generations later, He would still remind them. He even set up systems in which children would naturally ask their parents what something signified. The parents would recount God's works when the children inquired about the stones; or asked about the Passover or the other holy days that were set up. Jesus even instituted this for us in the Lord's Supper, "This is my body given for you; do this in remembrance of me (Luke 22:16 NIV)." Memorialize what you know that God is telling you right now. Do not delay. Look back on it often.

When you feel that you are under attack and you are questioning the fact that God actually called you to do what you felt so clearly previously, and looking at the memorialization is not reigniting the spark you once felt, it is time for obedience. You knew at one time that God had called you to some act of service. And yet now you are questioning that very calling. You are wondering if you heard him correctly.

- Did God really say that I am supposed to start this new career?
- Did God really say that I am supposed to write this book?
- Does God really say that I am supposed to do devotionals everyday with my children?
- Did God really say that I am supposed to try to figure out my husband's love language and love him unconditionally every day despite his behavior?
- Did God really say?

If your questions start with, "Did God really say," and at one point in time you were confident in what God called you to do, then you can be sure that your thought is not from God but from Satan. It is at this time that you need to walk in obedience. Simply continue doing what you know God called you to do in the beginning, and even if your feelings have not caught up with your actions yet, you will succeed. This book and our website and ministry are simply acts of obedience. I have doubted myself and doubted others and doubted God's call over and over again throughout all of this. However, I am confident in the initial call; therefore, I put one foot in front of the other and remain simply obedient.

Do not fear when you doubt. Do not despair when you question God's call. Do not throw in the towel over obstacles. Do not cower when others criticize your efforts. Do not give in. God does not make mistakes and His word does not return void (Isaiah 55:11). Memorialize His call on your life, and simply obey.

SATAN WANTS YOU TO QUESTION GOD'S CALL ON YOUR LIFE. HE WANTS YOU TO GIVE IN TO THOUGHTS THAT QUESTION GOD'S GOODNESS, SOVEREIGNTY, AND OMNIPOTENCE. HE WANTS TO DERAIL THE PROGRESS THAT YOU ARE MAKING. HE WANTS TO PUT A WRENCH IN ALL YOU DO SO YOU FEEL MORE LIKE A FAILURE THAN A FOLLOWER. IF HE CAN TWIST YOUR THINKING TO DOUBT THAT YOU HEARD GOD CORRECTLY IN ONE AREA OF YOUR LIFE, HE WILL GAIN SOME GROUND AND BE ABLE TO MORE EASILY AFFECT OTHER AREAS OF YOUR LIFE.

BUT GOD WANTS YOU TO ADMIT YOUR FRAILTY AND ACKNOWLEDGE THAT IT'S NOT BY YOUR MIGHT, POWER OR STRENGTH BUT BY *HIS SPIRIT ALONE* (ZECHARIAH 4:6)! HE IS FAITHFUL. PHILIPPIANS 1:6 SAYS, "HE WHO BEGAN A GOOD WORK IN YOU WILL CARRY IT ON TO COMPLETION UNTIL THE DAY OF CHRIST JESUS (NIV)." GOD DOES NOT GIVE UP ON WHAT HE STARTS IN YOU. REMEMBER HIS CALLING. MEMORIALIZE IT AND TELL OTHERS ABOUT IT OFTEN! WHEN ALL ELSE FAILS, "PRESS ON TOWARD THE GOAL TO WIN THE PRIZE FOR WHICH GOD HAS CALLED [YOU] HEAVENWARD IN CHRIST JESUS" AND DO NOT TURN YOUR BACK ON YOUR CALLING OR THROW IN THE TOWEL (PHILIPPIANS 3:14 NIV).

Chapter 5

The Lord is With You

Satan wants you to doubt God's presence and reign over your circumstances.
BUT GOD wants you know that He, as a completely trustworthy LORD, has been with you your whole life and will never leave you.

Genesis 37:36, 39:1-6

Meanwhile, the Midianites sold Joseph in Egypt to Potiphar, one of Pharaoh's officials, the captain of the guard. Now Joseph had been taken down to Egypt. Potiphar, an Egyptian who was one of Pharaoh's officials, the captain of the guard, bought him from the Ishmaelites who had taken him there. The Lord was with Joseph so that he prospered, and he lived in the house of his Egyptian master. When his master saw that the Lord was with him and that the Lord gave him success in everything he did, Joseph found favor in his eyes and became his attendant. Potiphar put him in charge of his household, and he entrusted to his care everything he owned. From the time he put him in charge of his household and of all that he owned, the Lord blessed the household of the Egyptian because of Joseph. The blessing of the Lord was on everything Potiphar had, both in the house and in the field. So Potiphar left everything he had in Joseph's care; with Joseph in charge, he did not concern himself with anything except the food he ate (NIV).

The phrase "the LORD was with Joseph [or him]" occurs four times in twenty-three verses. This is the central idea of this story. Despite what happened to Joseph, God was right there with him. Despite being a slave, "Joseph found favor in the eyes" of Potiphar (Genesis 39:4). Despite hitting rock bottom, God allowed Joseph to prosper within the household of his master, Potiphar; so much so, that Potiphar noticed and put him in charge of the entire household! It says that Potiphar "saw that the Lord was with [Joseph] and that the Lord gave him success in everything he did." Once Joseph was put in charge of Potiphar's household, it says that "the Lord blessed the household because of Joseph." God wants us to know that He can cause miracles to happen all around even when we hit rock bottom and despite this, others around us can see that the Lord is with us too, so through our circumstances God can bless others!

Maybe you are facing a situation where you are so depressed, discouraged, lonely and abandoned that you can barely muster the courage to pray. Maybe you have been so entangled in sin that you cannot possibly see how to "right the wrong." Maybe you have been so wounded by others that you cannot possibly think of trusting God whom you cannot see because those of whom you can see have failed you time and time again. Maybe it is an illness, mental or physical, that has taken its toll on you or a loved one.

You have prayed but have not seen any answers. You still struggle with the same sins and doubts and fears. The pain is still there, the hurt is still there, the memories are still there. Where is God in this time of torture? Is there a light at the end of the tunnel? Will things ever get better? Will you ever be whole again?

It is during these times when we feel so distant from the Lord, that He can do mighty works. He can make you prosper. Despite your slavery to sin, He can hold your head up high because of the salvation that He offers. Despite your circumstances He can bless your efforts and cause other people to see Him through it. Even if it is difficult for you to see Him through your circumstances, others can see how He is at work in the events in your life. This can be a time of increased blessing. The scripture does not say that Joseph recognized that the Lord was with him, it says Potiphar recognized that the Lord was with Joseph. That is important. You may not see God's hand in it but other people might be able to see that and possibly speak into your life. Ask somebody where they see God working in you and through you. That might just give you the encouragement you need to put one foot in front of the other.

When you are wrestling whether God is with you or not, it is very helpful to make a list of all the ways you have seen Him at work over the course of your life. We will touch on this a little more in a later chapter, but writing out where you have seen God's trustworthiness will help you to see that He has, in fact always been there. Even when you did not know it and did not ask for Him to be there. You can see how He was there.

When I struggle with anxiety and my thoughts start to spiral, I look back at my list. At the very beginning is, "I'm not supposed to be alive, but God protected me in my mother's womb and therefore, He can be trusted." My biological mother used many drugs when she was pregnant with me. She was also in an abusive relationship with a man who had caused a few miscarriages previously due to the beatings. She even had some abortions. It is clear to see that my birth was a miracle. I can trust God because I never asked for protection. I never asked for different circumstances. God was faithful and acted on His holy will. He was with me every step of the way and He is with you too!

SATAN WANTS YOU TO QUESTION WHETHER GOD IS WITH YOU AT ALL. HE WANTS YOU TO GIVE IN TO DESPAIR, FEAR AND ANXIETY. HE WANTS YOU TO BE AFRAID AND THINK THAT GOD HAS ABANDONED YOU. HE WANTS YOU TO THINK THAT IF GOD WAS WITH YOU, YOUR CIRCUMSTANCES WOULD BE DIFFERENT.

BUT GOD WANTS YOU TO SEE HOW HE HAS BEEN GRACIOUS AND FAITHFUL TO YOU OVER YOUR ENTIRE EXISTENCE. GOD WANTS TO SPEAK TO YOU AS HE INSTRUCTED MOSES TO SPEAK TO JOSHUA IN DEUTERONOMY 31:8. HE WANTS YOU TO KNOW THAT HE, THE LORD, GOES BEFORE YOU IN EVERYTHING THAT CROSSES YOUR PATH. HE WILL NOT LEAVE YOU ALONE AND HE WILL NOT TURN HIS BACK ON YOU, EVER. HE DOES NOT WANT YOU TO FEAR OR BE DISCOURAGED. SO BE COURAGEOUS IN ALL CIRCUMSTANCES BECAUSE YOU CAN HAVE FAITH IN A TRUSTWORTHY GOD.

Chapter 6

When You Are Tempted

Satan wants to stunt your impact in this life, so he sends you craftily devised temptations that are uniquely tailored to you, hoping you will give in and let the sin ruin you - and what does not ruin you, he will try to crush you with the weight of the guilt that follows.
BUT GOD wants you to understand your Enemy's tactics and be diligent and alert, so you know when to flee, but if you do give in, He also wants you to know that He is in the business of restoration and redemption.

Genesis 39:6b-20a

Now Joseph was well-built and handsome, and after a while his master's wife took notice of Joseph and said, "Come to bed with me!" But he refused. "With me in charge," he told her, "my master does not concern himself with anything in the house; everything he owns he has entrusted to my care. No one is greater in this house than I am. My master has withheld nothing from me except you, because you are his wife. How then could I do such a wicked thing and sin against God?" And though she spoke to Joseph day after day, he refused to go to bed with her or even be with her. One day he went into the house to attend to his duties, and none of the household servants was inside. She caught him by his cloak and said, "Come to bed with me!" But he left his cloak in her hand and ran out of the house. When she saw that he had left his cloak in her hand and had run out of the house, she called her household servants. "Look," she said to them, "this Hebrew has been brought to us to make sport of us! He came in here to sleep with me, but I screamed. When he heard me scream for help, he left his cloak beside me and ran out of the house." She kept his cloak beside her until his master came home. Then she told him this story: "That Hebrew slave you brought us came to me to make sport of me. But as soon as I screamed for help, he left his cloak beside me and ran out of the house." When his master heard the story his wife told him, saying, "This is how your slave treated me," he burned with anger. Joseph's master took him and put him in prison, the place where the king's prisoners were confined (NIV).

False accusations are hurtful. Joseph was an honorable man. He was a man who feared God and sought the best for his master. He was faithful in his duties and did not neglect them even though he was pursued by the master's wife. He kept doing what God had called him to do in that moment. He did not falter.

No matter what situation you are called into, whether it would be a devastating circumstance or an ordinary day, you will experience temptation. We are all tempted every day, just like Joseph. We are tempted in the little things and tempted in the big things. Sometimes you are tempted to lose your temper. Other times we are tempted to turn our backs on the ones that we love. Sometimes we are tempted to be selfish and seek pleasure and leisure in destructive places. We long to get back at the people who have hurt us and make them pay for their words or actions; we seek *our* justice. The last word must be ours. We want to make sure everyone knows that we are right. Affirmation and acceptance become idols in our lives. We make excuses to cover up our own laziness, trying to save face without actually doing anything. We cling tightly to self-preservation. We seek our own way above God's.

The Tempter will tempt you. He will pull out everything in his arsenal in order to try to trip you up. It is difficult to withstand the pressure. He will come to you when your defenses are down and your resolve is weak. Give him an inch in those moments of frailty and your self-control will begin to crumble. Joseph never gave an inch. Scripture says, "he refused to go to bed with her or *even be with her* (Gen. 39:10 NIV emphasis mine)." You cannot engage the devil as Eve did. You cannot have a conversation with him. You must refuse and resist him in the name of Jesus. Not only did Joseph refuse, but he also avoided contact. James 4:7b says, "Resist the devil, and he will flee from you (NLT)."

The Lord is with you during these times of temptation. When you are tired from being up all night with a sick child and your reserves are down, the Lord is with you. You will be tempted to have a quick temper and snarky remarks to a husband who says, "I don't know why you don't just go to bed earlier." When your husband rarely notices your new haircut and forgets your anniversary, you may be tempted to give into the co-worker who gives you his full attention, God is there with you. When you have lost a loved one, but you have to carry on with life, you may be tempted to retreat inward and push others away, God is there with you.

1 Corinthians 10:13 says, "No temptation has overtaken you that is not common to man. God is faithful, and he will not let you be tempted beyond your ability, but with the temptation he will also provide the way of escape, that you may be able to endure it (ESV)." He provided Joseph a way of escape: prison! The Lord will strengthen you so you can hold up under the pressure. 1 Peter 5:8-9 says, "Be alert and of sober mind. Your enemy the devil prowls around like a roaring lion looking for someone to devour. Resist him, standing firm in the faith, because you know that the family of believers throughout the world is undergoing the same kind of sufferings (NIV)." God will be with you through whatever circumstances and temptations you may be facing. He is "for" you and longs for your success. Partner with Him on your knees.

But what if you've already succumbed to temptation? You are filled with guilt and shame. You did not flee. You engaged and then your resolve left you. You were not able to withstand. God was with you then and He is with you now. He longs for you to turn your heart toward Him, repent and enter into the safety of His mercy. You are loved. There is nothing you can do that is beyond God's grace. A great place to start is meditating on Psalm 51:1-17 and Psalm 32. Let the words sink deep into your soul. When the guilt rises again, look at these verses. God will not despise you; blessed are you whose sins are forgiven!

Psalm 51

Have mercy on me, O God,
according to your unfailing love;
according to your great compassion
blot out my transgressions.
Wash away all my iniquity
and cleanse me from my sin.

For I know my transgressions,
and my sin is always before me.
Against you, you only, have I sinned
and done what is evil in your sight;
so you are right in your verdict
and justified when you judge.
Surely I was sinful at birth,
sinful from the time my mother conceived me.
Yet you desired faithfulness even in the womb;
you taught me wisdom in that secret place.

Cleanse me with hyssop, and I will be clean;
wash me, and I will be whiter than snow.
Let me hear joy and gladness;
let the bones you have crushed rejoice.
Hide your face from my sins
and blot out all my iniquity.

Create in me a pure heart, O God,
and renew a steadfast spirit within me.
Do not cast me from your presence
or take your Holy Spirit from me.
Restore to me the joy of your salvation
and grant me a willing spirit, to sustain me.

Then I will teach transgressors your ways,
so that sinners will turn back to you.
Deliver me from the guilt of bloodshed, O God,
you who are God my Savior,

and my tongue will sing of your righteousness.
Open my lips, Lord,
and my mouth will declare your praise.
You do not delight in sacrifice, or I would bring it;
you do not take pleasure in burnt offerings.
My sacrifice, O God, is a broken spirit;
a broken and contrite heart
you, God, will not despise (NIV).

Psalm 32

Blessed is the one
whose transgressions are forgiven,
whose sins are covered.
Blessed is the one
Whose sin the LORD does not count against them
and in whose spirit is no deceit.

When I kept silent,
my bones wasted away
through my groaning all day long.
For day and night
your hand was heavy on me;
my strength was sapped
as in the heat of summer.

Then I acknowledged my sin to you
and did not cover up my iniquity.
I said, "I will confess
my transgressions to the LORD."
And you forgave
the guilt of my sin.

Therefore let all the faithful pray to you
while you may be found;
surely the rising of the mighty waters
will not reach them.
You are my hiding place;
you will protect me from trouble
and surround me with songs of deliverance.

I will instruct you and teach you in the way you should go;
I will counsel you with my loving eye on you.
Do not be like the horse or the mule,
which have no understanding
but must be controlled by bit and bridle
or they will not come to you.
Many are the woes of the wicked,
but the LORD's unfailing love
surrounds the one who trusts in him.

Rejoice in the LORD and be glad, you righteous;
sing, all you who are upright in heart! (NIV)

While the Lord wants you to flee from your Enemy, if you happen to succumb, God can still use that ugliness and turn it into something beautiful. You can help others turn back to the Lord. The Lord will deliver you from the guilt and shame of sin so that you can rest in Him as Savior and sing of His righteousness. Through God's power displayed in weakness, He will open your lips. You won't be afraid to proclaim how He has worked. His praise will always be on your lips.

SATAN WANTS YOU TO GIVE IN TO TEMPTATION, PLAIN AND SIMPLE. HE WANTS YOU TO FAIL SO HE CAN ACCUSE YOU BEFORE YOUR MAKER. HE IS A LIAR THAT TELLS YOU YOUR PRESENT CHOICE WON'T MATTER IN THE FUTURE. HE TELLS YOU THAT YOU CANNOT POSSIBLY WITHSTAND THE PRESSURE, SO YOU MAY AS WELL GIVE IN. HE KNOWS EXACTLY HOW TO ATTACK YOU. HE EXPLOITS YOUR EGO, SELF-CONSCIOUSNESS, FEELINGS OF INADEQUACY, FEARS AND EVEN YOUR DREAMS, GIFTS AND DEEPEST LONGINGS. ONCE HE SUCCEEDS IN HIS TEMPTATIONS, HE THEN PROCEEDS TO TELL YOU THAT GOD CANNOT FORGIVE YOU.

BUT GOD WANTS YOU TO KNOW THAT HE IS ALWAYS WITH YOU, HELPING YOU WITHSTAND THE TEMPTATIONS THROWN AT YOU. HE WILL NEVER DESPISE YOU WHEN YOU COME TO HIM WITH

REGRET FROM YOUR SINS. HE DOES NOT WANT YOU TO KEEP SILENT ABOUT YOUR SINS. BY TELLING OTHERS ABOUT THEM AND HOW GOD TOOK BACK THE GROUND IN YOUR HEART THAT YOU HAD GIVEN TO THE ENEMY, YOU CAN STRENGTHEN OTHERS AND HELP THEM SEE THEIR ESCAPE ROUTES. HE WILL FORGIVE YOU AND WELCOME YOU INTO HIS LOVING EMBRACE. EVERY SINGLE TIME. EVERY SINGLE DAY. FOR THE REST OF YOUR LIFE.

STOP! BEFORE YOU GO ANY FURTHER, ACCESS THE **FREE, DOWNLOADABLE** *Study Guide* HERE:

http://visitor.r20.constantcontact.com/d.jsp?llr=qyarwexab&p=oi&m=1124365533968&sit=z7tlokqkb&f=8298aefb-3e02-419e-b440-610589fe255a

Chapter 7
Taking a Concentrated Break

Satan wants you to think you are too busy to sit in concentrated spiritual development and will try his best to orchestrate your circumstances to cloud your thinking.

BUT GOD wants you to shut out the outside world and take a concentrated rest, or Sabbath, from all things peripheral so that He can work on spiritual discipline and character development to shape you into the person He created you to be.

Genesis 39:20b-23

But while Joseph was there in the prison, the Lord was with him; he showed him kindness and granted him favor in the eyes of the prison warden. So the warden put Joseph in charge of all those held in the prison, and he was made responsible for all that was done there. The warden paid no attention to anything under Joseph's care, because the Lord was with Joseph and gave him success in whatever he did (NIV).

It says that the Lord gave Joseph "success in whatever he did (verse 23 NIV)." That applies to the physical acts he performed. It must have applied to his prayer life as well. I can imagine him crying out to God to reveal Himself. Have you ever cried that before: "God where are you? Please just let me see you! Do not turn your back on me. I can endure anything as long as you are with me. Please let me know you are here!" I am sure he prayed for and against his brothers and Potiphar's wife as well. Have you ever been faced with such betrayal that it was difficult to forgive a person? Joseph must have struggled with forgiveness a bit during his confinement and it is here where God prepared his heart to encounter his brothers once again. God allowed this time of concentrated focus in Joseph's life to perfect His grace in Joseph's weakness.

An intense time of forgetting about all outside things and focusing on your relationship with God is needed every now and then. We need to take Sabbaths. Joseph was not in a time of Sabbath rest exactly, but the outside world was out of reach, so he could only concern himself with whom he had control over. No outside pressures, just himself and the other prisoners. There is something to be said about concentrated emphasis on your relationship with God and your relationship with the people with whom you live (more on this next chapter).

During these times of seclusion meditating on Scripture is of utmost importance. Getting perspective on what God says and how His infallible words pertain to you has infinite value. Psalm 119 is a fantastic meditation for rerouting your thinking away from the cares of this world and toward God's precepts. Although written centuries later, as you read this, you can almost picture Joseph crying out to God using many of these words:

א Aleph

Blessed are those whose ways are blameless,
who walk according to the law of the LORD.
Blessed are those who keep his statutes
and seek him with all their heart—
they do no wrong
but follow his ways.
You have laid down precepts
that are to be fully obeyed.
Oh, that my ways were steadfast
in obeying your decrees!
Then I would not be put to shame
when I consider all your commands.
I will praise you with an upright heart
as I learn your righteous laws.
I will obey your decrees;
do not utterly forsake me.

ב Beth

How can a young person stay on the path of purity?
By living according to your word.

I seek you with all my heart;
do not let me stray from your commands.
I have hidden your word in my heart
that I might not sin against you.
Praise be to you, LORD;
teach me your decrees.
With my lips I recount
all the laws that come from your mouth.
I rejoice in following your statutes
as one rejoices in great riches.
I meditate on your precepts
and consider your ways.
I delight in your decrees;
I will not neglect your word.

ג Gimel

Be good to your servant while I live,
that I may obey your word.
Open my eyes that I may see
wonderful things in your law.
I am a stranger on earth;
do not hide your commands from me.
My soul is consumed with longing
for your laws at all times.
You rebuke the arrogant, who are accursed,
those who stray from your commands.
Remove from me their scorn and contempt,
for I keep your statutes.
Though rulers sit together and slander me,
your servant will meditate on your decrees.
Your statutes are my delight;
they are my counselors.

ד Daleth

I am laid low in the dust;
preserve my life according to your word.
I gave an account of my ways and you answered me;
teach me your decrees.
Cause me to understand the way of your precepts,
that I may meditate on your wonderful deeds.
My soul is weary with sorrow;

strengthen me according to your word.
Keep me from deceitful ways;
be gracious to me and teach me your law.
I have chosen the way of faithfulness;
I have set my heart on your laws.
I hold fast to your statutes, LORD;
do not let me be put to shame.
I run in the path of your commands,
for you have broadened my understanding.

ה He

Teach me, LORD, the way of your decrees,
that I may follow it to the end.
Give me understanding, so that I may keep your law
and obey it with all my heart.
Direct me in the path of your commands,
for there I find delight.
Turn my heart toward your statutes
and not toward selfish gain.
Turn my eyes away from worthless things;
preserve my life according to your word.
Fulfill your promise to your servant,
so that you may be feared.
Take away the disgrace I dread,
for your laws are good.
How I long for your precepts!
In your righteousness preserve my life.

ו Waw

May your unfailing love come to me, LORD,
your salvation, according to your promise;
then I can answer anyone who taunts me,
for I trust in your word.
Never take your word of truth from my mouth,
for I have put my hope in your laws.
I will always obey your law,
for ever and ever.
I will walk about in freedom,
for I have sought out your precepts.
I will speak of your statutes before kings
and will not be put to shame,

for I delight in your commands
because I love them.
I reach out for your commands, which I love,
that I may meditate on your decrees.

ז Zayin

Remember your word to your servant,
for you have given me hope.
My comfort in my suffering is this:
Your promise preserves my life.
The arrogant mock me unmercifully,
but I do not turn from your law.
I remember, LORD, your ancient laws,
and I find comfort in them.
Indignation grips me because of the wicked,
who have forsaken your law.
Your decrees are the theme of my song
wherever I lodge.
In the night, LORD, I remember your name,
that I may keep your law.
This has been my practice:
I obey your precepts.

ח Heth

You are my portion, LORD;
I have promised to obey your words.
I have sought your face with all my heart;
be gracious to me according to your promise.
I have considered my ways
and have turned my steps to your statutes.
I will hasten and not delay
to obey your commands.
Though the wicked bind me with ropes,
I will not forget your law.
At midnight I rise to give you thanks
for your righteous laws.
I am a friend to all who fear you,
to all who follow your precepts.
The earth is filled with your love, LORD;
teach me your decrees.

ט Teth

Do good to your servant
according to your word, LORD.
Teach me knowledge and good judgment,
for I trust your commands.
Before I was afflicted I went astray,
but now I obey your word.
You are good, and what you do is good;
teach me your decrees.
Though the arrogant have smeared me with lies,
I keep your precepts with all my heart.
Their hearts are callous and unfeeling,
but I delight in your law.
It was good for me to be afflicted
so that I might learn your decrees.
The law from your mouth is more precious to me
than thousands of pieces of silver and gold.

              ׳ Yodh

Your hands made me and formed me;
give me understanding to learn your commands.
May those who fear you rejoice when they see me,
for I have put my hope in your word.
I know, LORD, that your laws are righteous,
and that in faithfulness you have afflicted me.
May your unfailing love be my comfort,
according to your promise to your servant.
Let your compassion come to me that I may live,
for your law is my delight.
May the arrogant be put to shame for wronging me without cause;
but I will meditate on your precepts.
May those who fear you turn to me,
those who understand your statutes.
May I wholeheartedly follow your decrees,
that I may not be put to shame.

              כ Kaph

My soul faints with longing for your salvation,
but I have put my hope in your word.
My eyes fail, looking for your promise;
I say, "When will you comfort me?"
Though I am like a wineskin in the smoke,

I do not forget your decrees.
How long must your servant wait?
When will you punish my persecutors?
The arrogant dig pits to trap me,
contrary to your law.
All your commands are trustworthy;
help me, for I am being persecuted without cause.
They almost wiped me from the earth,
but I have not forsaken your precepts.
In your unfailing love preserve my life,
that I may obey the statutes of your mouth.

ל Lamedh

Your word, LORD, is eternal;
it stands firm in the heavens.
Your faithfulness continues through all generations;
you established the earth, and it endures.
Your laws endure to this day,
for all things serve you.
If your law had not been my delight,
I would have perished in my affliction.
I will never forget your precepts,
for by them you have preserved my life.
Save me, for I am yours;
I have sought out your precepts.
The wicked are waiting to destroy me,
but I will ponder your statutes.
To all perfection I see a limit,
but your commands are boundless.

מ Mem

Oh, how I love your law!
I meditate on it all day long.
Your commands are always with me
and make me wiser than my enemies.
I have more insight than all my teachers,
for I meditate on your statutes.
I have more understanding than the elders,
for I obey your precepts.
I have kept my feet from every evil path
so that I might obey your word.

I have not departed from your laws,
for you yourself have taught me.
How sweet are your words to my taste,
sweeter than honey to my mouth!
I gain understanding from your precepts;
therefore I hate every wrong path.

נ Nun

Your word is a lamp for my feet,
a light on my path.
I have taken an oath and confirmed it,
that I will follow your righteous laws.
I have suffered much;
preserve my life, LORD, according to your word.
Accept, LORD, the willing praise of my mouth,
and teach me your laws.
Though I constantly take my life in my hands,
I will not forget your law.
The wicked have set a snare for me,
but I have not strayed from your precepts.
Your statutes are my heritage forever;
they are the joy of my heart.
My heart is set on keeping your decrees
to the very end.

ס Samekh

I hate double-minded people,
but I love your law.
You are my refuge and my shield;
I have put my hope in your word.
Away from me, you evildoers,
that I may keep the commands of my God!
Sustain me, my God, according to your promise, and I will live;
do not let my hopes be dashed.
Uphold me, and I will be delivered;
I will always have regard for your decrees.
You reject all who stray from your decrees,
for their delusions come to nothing.
All the wicked of the earth you discard like dross;
therefore I love your statutes.
My flesh trembles in fear of you;

I stand in awe of your laws.

ע Ayin

I have done what is righteous and just;
do not leave me to my oppressors.
Ensure your servant's well-being;
do not let the arrogant oppress me.
My eyes fail, looking for your salvation,
looking for your righteous promise.
Deal with your servant according to your love
and teach me your decrees.
I am your servant; give me discernment
that I may understand your statutes.
It is time for you to act, LORD;
your law is being broken.
Because I love your commands
more than gold, more than pure gold,
and because I consider all your precepts right,
I hate every wrong path.

פ Pe

Your statutes are wonderful;
therefore I obey them.
The unfolding of your words gives light;
it gives understanding to the simple.
I open my mouth and pant,
longing for your commands.
Turn to me and have mercy on me,
as you always do to those who love your name.
Direct my footsteps according to your word;
let no sin rule over me.
Redeem me from human oppression,
that I may obey your precepts.
Make your face shine on your servant
and teach me your decrees.
Streams of tears flow from my eyes,
for your law is not obeyed.

צ Tsadhe

You are righteous, LORD,
and your laws are right.
The statutes you have laid down are righteous;

they are fully trustworthy.
My zeal wears me out,
for my enemies ignore your words.
Your promises have been thoroughly tested,
and your servant loves them.
Though I am lowly and despised,
I do not forget your precepts.
Your righteousness is everlasting
and your law is true.
Trouble and distress have come upon me,
but your commands give me delight.
Your statutes are always righteous;
give me understanding that I may live.

ק Qoph

I call with all my heart; answer me, LORD,
and I will obey your decrees.
I call out to you; save me
and I will keep your statutes.
I rise before dawn and cry for help;
I have put my hope in your word.
My eyes stay open through the watches of the night,
that I may meditate on your promises.
Hear my voice in accordance with your love;
preserve my life, LORD, according to your laws.
Those who devise wicked schemes are near,
but they are far from your law.
Yet you are near, LORD,
and all your commands are true.
Long ago I learned from your statutes
that you established them to last forever.

ר Resh

Look on my suffering and deliver me,
for I have not forgotten your law.
Defend my cause and redeem me;
preserve my life according to your promise.
Salvation is far from the wicked,
for they do not seek out your decrees.
Your compassion, LORD, is great;
preserve my life according to your laws.

Many are the foes who persecute me,
but I have not turned from your statutes.
I look on the faithless with loathing,
for they do not obey your word.
See how I love your precepts;
preserve my life, LORD, in accordance with your love.
All your words are true;
all your righteous laws are eternal.

ש Sin and Shin

Rulers persecute me without cause,
but my heart trembles at your word.
I rejoice in your promise
like one who finds great spoil.
I hate and detest falsehood
but I love your law.
Seven times a day I praise you
for your righteous laws.
Great peace have those who love your law,
and nothing can make them stumble.
I wait for your salvation, LORD,
and I follow your commands.
I obey your statutes,
for I love them greatly.
I obey your precepts and your statutes,
for all my ways are known to you.

ת Taw

May my cry come before you, LORD;
give me understanding according to your word.
May my supplication come before you;
deliver me according to your promise.
May my lips overflow with praise,
for you teach me your decrees.
May my tongue sing of your word,
for all your commands are righteous.
May your hand be ready to help me,
for I have chosen your precepts.
I long for your salvation, LORD,
and your law gives me delight.
Let me live that I may praise you,

and may your laws sustain me.
I have strayed like a lost sheep.
Seek your servant,
for I have not forgotten your commands (NIV).

Get to know yourself while you are taking time away from the outside world. Understand your strengths (see next chapter) and weaknesses. What is your personality style and how does that help and hinder your relationships? How can you live in your strengths? God created you specifically for this day and for this hour. What is holding you back from living in light of how He created you? Where can you improve your attitude, responses and reactions? God's word says, "My grace is sufficient for you, for my power is made perfect in weakness.' Therefore I will boast all the more gladly about my weaknesses, so that Christ's power may rest on me (2 Cor 12:9 NIV)." God can take your weakness, humble you in them and use them for His glory. Nothing is impossible for Him! He can make it so that your fear or anxiety are used to help minister to others! Your temper can be tempered. Your inability to establish boundaries can help serve others. God never leaves you in your weaknesses. He's there with you through it all and He can help you conquer what you need to overcome, and alter what you need to change. His power is perfected and manifested through your weaknesses and what He does through them for His glory. You may never fully master what you've been working on in this lifetime. However, it is through the trial of working on that weakness that God can perform miracles inside your heart and in the hearts of others. Look for opportunities to be vulnerable and share those weaknesses with others and glean tips from them and help them on their journey.

If you do not take the time to unplug and stop chasing after the things of this world, you will never be still long enough for God to do some intense work on your character. You've got to be intentional in setting aside time and creating a Sabbath so you can be silent, be still and be surrendered to what God has to say. God will use that time of "seclusion" and help develop you into the person He will use to help others. Even Paul had a time of seclusion before he went into full-time ministry. Galatians 1:15-18 says, "But when

God, who set me apart from my mother's womb and called me by his grace, was pleased to reveal his Son in me so that I might preach him among the Gentiles, my immediate response was not to consult any human being. I did not go up to Jerusalem to see those who were apostles before I was, but I went into Arabia. Later I returned to Damascus. Then after three years, I went up to Jerusalem to get acquainted with Cephas and stayed with him fifteen days (NIV)." God used this intense time of learning in Arabia to show Paul who He wanted him to be: a minister of the Gospel to the Gentiles. You must take the time to get rid of as much outside influence as you can so that you can hear God's Spirit tell you who He has created you to be and how He wants you to live that out.

SATAN WANTS YOU TO BE SO BUSY THAT YOU CANNOT SEE THE HOPE OF A SITUATION. HE WANTS YOU TO BE ONLY CONSUMED BY YOUR CIRCUMSTANCE. YOUR WEAKNESSES WILL ALWAYS BE THERE AND THERE'S NO HOPE IN CHANGING THEM. EVEN WHEN YOU RESOLVE TO SPEND IN DEPTH TIME WITH THE LORD TO WORK ON YOURSELF, SATAN WILL CONVINCE YOU THAT YOU ARE FAR TOO BUSY. YOU WILL FIND THAT YOUR CALENDAR FILLS UP QUICKLY AND YOU WILL HARDLY HAVE ANY BREATHING ROOM.

BUT GOD WANTS YOU TO KNOW THAT EVERY OPPORTUNITY IS A TRAINING OPPORTUNITY. HE CAN CAUSE BEAUTY TO RISE OUT OF THE ASHES. HE WANTS YOU TO BE STILL LONG ENOUGH SO YOU TWO CAN INTENSELY WORK ON THIS TOGETHER. THAT TAKES INTENTIONALITY AND A WILLINGNESS TO LET GO OF THE OUTSIDE THINGS THAT PULL YOU IN DIFFERENT DIRECTIONS. IT ALSO REQUIRES A RELINQUISHING OF CONTROL TO OTHERS AS WELL AS TO GOD TO ORCHESTRATE AND TIME THINGS PERFECTLY. YOU MUST LEARN TO SAY, "NO," TO THE OUTSIDE WORLD AND QUITE POSSIBLY SOME REALLY NOBLE ACTIVITIES OR CAUSES. BUT NONE OF THOSE WILL EVER COMPARE TO THE INTENSE CHARACTER DEVELOPMENT GOD LONGS TO ACCOMPLISH IN YOUR HEART.

Chapter 8

Live in Your Strengths

Satan does not want you to take the time to understand the people God has placed in your life; he wants you to live in your weaknesses and think God has made a mistake in how He designed you.
BUT GOD wants you to take the time to be a student of others; He wants you to live in your strengths assured that He created you with intentionality and He can exhibit His strength in your weaknesses.

Genesis 40:1-22

Some time later, the cupbearer and the baker of the king of Egypt offended their master, the king of Egypt. Pharaoh was angry with his two officials, the chief cupbearer and the chief baker, and put them in custody in the house of the captain of the guard, in the same prison where Joseph was confined. The captain of the guard assigned them to Joseph, and he attended them. After they had been in custody for some time, each of the two men—the cupbearer and the baker of the king of Egypt, who were being held in prison—had a dream the same night, and each dream had a meaning of its own. *When Joseph came to them the next morning, he saw that they were dejected. So he asked Pharaoh's officials who were in custody with him in his master's house, "Why do you look so sad today?"* "We both had dreams," they answered, "but there is no one to interpret them." Then Joseph said to them, "Do not interpretations belong to God? Tell me your dreams." So the chief cupbearer told Joseph his dream. He said to him, "In my dream I saw a vine in front of me, and on the vine were three branches. As soon as it budded, it blossomed, and its clusters ripened into grapes. Pharaoh's cup was in my hand, and I took the grapes, squeezed them into Pharaoh's cup and put the cup in his hand."   "This is what it means," Joseph said to him. "The three branches are three days. Within three days Pharaoh will lift up your head and restore you to your position, and you will put Pharaoh's cup in his hand, just as you used to do when you were his cupbearer. But when all goes well with you, remember me and show me kindness; mention me to Pharaoh and get me out of this prison. I was forcibly carried off from the land of the Hebrews, and even here I have done nothing to deserve being put in a dungeon." When the chief baker saw that Joseph had given a favorable interpretation, he said to Joseph, "I too had a dream: On my head were three baskets of bread. In the top basket were all kinds of baked goods for Pharaoh, but the birds were eating them out of the basket on my head." "This is what it means," Joseph said. "The three baskets are three days. Within three days Pharaoh will lift off your head and impale your body on a pole. And the birds will eat away your flesh." Now the third day was Pharaoh's birthday, and he gave a feast for all his officials. He lifted up the heads of the chief cupbearer and the chief baker in the presence of his officials: He restored the chief cupbearer to his position, so that he once again put the cup into Pharaoh's hand— but he impaled the chief baker, just as Joseph had said to them in his interpretation (NIV).

This is a long passage, so I highlighted the verses that contain the themes with which we will concern ourselves. We see here that Joseph was good at his job. He was in charge of the prisoners and he knew these prisoners well enough to see that they were sad about something. He was aware of the people under his care. He also knew himself well enough and lived in his strengths to know how he could help.

Get to know the people under your care: co-workers, children, husband, parents, volunteers, students...etc. Know what helps them succeed. They look to you for guidance and nurturing. Learn how best to minister to them. How do they learn? When you figure out how they learn, you can better communicate your needs and their instructions to them. What motivates them? What discourages them? You need to be a student of those around you so you can serve them best and help them succeed. Joseph knew immediately that the people under his care were upset.

- Do you take time from your busy life to know when someone is upset around you?
- Do you enter into their pain and inquire about how to help them through whatever it is that is bothering them or do you have only good intentions?
- Do you intend to help them along and then get caught up in your day to day tasks and completely forget? You missed a God given opportunity to follow His will.

In an interview with Dr. Gary Chapman on *Building Relationships*, Dr. Kathy Koch outlined what she calls the "8 great smarts" that are within each and every one of us.   Each child has all of the "smarts" as she calls them, but each one has to be awakened. The "8 great smarts" are: Logic Smart, Self Smart, Nature Smart, Music Smart, Body Smart, People Smart, Picture Smart and Word Smart. It is up to us as parents, educators and people of influence to set up scenarios in which these "smarts" can be awakened.

You can use this to evaluate everyone in your sphere of influence and set them up to live within their strengths. When it comes to my children, I found one way to do this was to pay attention to how they get in trouble. My daughter is constantly humming and singing. She is never without a song on her lips. I am coming to understand that she is music smart.   I can be irritated with it or I can put on music when she's singing incessantly and join in with her! Check out where your children get in trouble: do they talk a lot in school? Is your son physical and is constantly getting in trouble in the nursery for tackling people? Maybe he is "body smart." Not that he is using his body in a smart way, mind you, but he thinks and processes things physically. Does your daughter draw all over the wall in her room? Does your son constantly ask you questions - especially, "Why?" Perhaps he is "logic smart." These could all point to their "smarts" that need to be channeled into positive ways of expression.

Another beneficial resource is by Cynthia Ulrich Tobias, "Every Child Can Succeed." She walks you through how to evaluate learning styles, personality temperaments and how to set yourself as well as your child up for success in learning and processing life. Know your kids. To help you evaluate your child's styles, please see the accompanying **Joseph Study Guide.**

Ask God to reveal a life verse for your child, or anyone in your life that is on your heart. For example: I knew God wanted me to pray that my daughter would have wisdom beyond her years. Ever since she was born, I have been praying that for her. God revealed to me that I needed to look at Daniel and see how God worked in that book and pray those verses over my daughter. Her life verse is Daniel 12:3 "Those who are wise will shine like the brightness of the heavens, and those who lead many to righteousness, like the stars for ever and ever (NIV)." My first son's book is Joshua. God revealed to me that I pray that he is strong and courageous, a major theme in the book of Joshua. Every so often, I will read the book of Joshua and pray through it concerning my son. Lastly, God revealed to me to pray Micah 6:8 over my second son as I pray that he be a man of integrity. Micah 6:8b says, "And what does the LORD require of you? To act justly and to love mercy and to walk humbly with your God (NIV)." The themes in Micah, Ezra and Nehemiah are what I read when I need guidance from God concerning him. God will reveal what He wants you to pray about for each child. You will be amazed at how God will confirm your prayers. In the last few years, many people have independently told me that my daughter seems "wise beyond her years." The *exact* wording, I have been using for over a decade! God is gracious to confirm what I am praying! He will be gracious to you as well.

Think about your husband. Do you know what makes him have a heart for you? Do you know how he best understands love? You may be telling him that you love him, but because "words of affirmation" is not how he best communicates and understands love, he will not hear it and in some cases, conclude the opposite. Dr. Gary Chapman has an excellent resource called "The Five Love Languages," which can be instrumental in any relationship. When you learn how to communicate love to another person in a way that they can recognize it, their hearts are warmed and turned to you. Obviously, this is not a manipulation to ultimately get your own way, but a way to put your spouse above yourself and work toward making sure they know, without a doubt, you love them. Some spouses go years without truly feeling like the other spouse deeply loves them.   Your life was meant to live together as one, do not waste it miscommunicating something as fundamental as love.

The second idea we see in this passage is that Joseph knew himself and his strengths well enough to be able to interpret the dreams of the cupbearer and the baker. First and foremost, Joseph gives glory to God. "Every good and perfect gift is from above, coming down from the Father of the heavenly lights, who does not change like shifting shadows (James 1:17 NIV)." Joseph recognized that his ability to interpret the dreams could only come from God, the one who gave the dreams and the one who can ultimately sort out their meanings. Whatever gifts and talents you have are given from the Lord. It is up to you to figure out what those gifts and talents are and to use them to further God's kingdom. Wherever there is a need, wherever there is a hole you can fill, wherever God is leading you and prompting you, you have a responsibility and an obligation to use those gifts and talents in those situations. And if you are not, you are in direct defiance of the One who created you. First Corinthians 12:11 says, "It is the one and only Spirit who distributes all these gifts. He alone decides which gift each person should have (NLT)." He made you uniquely qualified to do what He's called you to do.

- What are your gifts?
- How can you use them?
- What are your passions?
- When do you most feel alive?
- About what topic do people usually seek your advice

"There are different kinds of gifts, but the same Spirit distributes them. There are different kinds of service, but the same Lord. There are different kinds of working, but in all of them and in everyone it is the same God at work. Now to each one the manifestation of the

Spirit is given for the common good. To one there is given through the Spirit a message of wisdom, to another a message of knowledge by means of the same Spirit, to another faith by the same Spirit, to another gifts of healing by that one Spirit, to another miraculous powers, to another prophecy, to another distinguishing between spirits, to another speaking in different kinds of tongues, and to still another the interpretation of tongues (1 Corinthians 12:4-11 NIV)." Do not be intimidated or afraid of your gifts and talents. God created you to be you and if you are ashamed of that, you are telling God that He doesn't know what He is doing. My daughter helped me see this point.

We talked in Chapter 3 on "Faith Testimonies" about a concern over the direction our children's school was taking. I told you about how my husband and I discussing the disturbing aspects of this situation ministered to my daughter. The second part of that story is how my daughter ministered to me. I was expressing my overwhelming concern in a way that was animated and full of Bible quotes and a deep conviction of the very treacherous path their Christian school was exploring. When I was done with my mini sermonette, I climbed off my soap box, took a breath and look at my surprised daughter.   After praying about this as a family and discussing it in front of our middle schooler, she said, "...These are important things and you aren't afraid to speak your faith. Mom, I think that God created you this way for situations like this."

It is hard for me to tell you exactly how that touched my soul. I have always been ashamed of myself. I am brash and bold and outspoken. I have always felt like less of a woman for possessing those traits. Studies on meekness always made me feel worse about myself because I just couldn't master that. When our first child was a girl I actually panicked because I did not want her growing up to be like me. I was never proud of the fact that I have been so outspoken and opinionated. I have been fairly confident that what I have spoken in the past has been truth, but barely any love or grace was used to season the truth. I have always lamented why I can't be like other women I see and admire. It has only been in the last few years, when I have intensely tried to figure out who God created me to be, that I have been more secure in how He created me. My sinfulness will always get in the way, but I know God can redeem all things and He did not make a mistake in making me. As I have grown in confidence of who God created me to be, I have still always felt like perhaps other people still wish that God had made me differently. It wasn't until my daughter was proud of the fact that God made me who I am that I have felt free to fully embrace it. In that one simple statement, God showed me that He knows what He is doing and can be trusted in how He made me. Again, the tendency to be sinful is always there. However, God is in the business of renewing my mind and restoring His purpose through me.

When I started looking at my passions, interests and talents, I realized that I am a lot like some of the Old Testament prophets, especially Nehemiah and Ezra. Because of this, I started to read those books with myself in mind. I begged God to show me why He put certain fires in my belly. That is the only way I can describe what happens to me. When I hear the Truth distorted something burns within me and it is like a physical fire. Through Scripture, various tests on Spiritual Gifts as well as Godly counsel I know a spiritual gift of mine is discernment. The more I read Ezra, Nehemiah and other prophetic books, the more God sweetly ministers to my heart and my soul that has been hurting for so many years, wondering why God made me the way that He made me. His Word sealed and confirmed His purpose in my life. I am supposed to speak out the truth - His truth. I am called to do that, and when I don't do that I am disobeying God. When I do speak out the truth, I can look to those books in the Bible as well as how Jesus communicated and used words. I am able to see how God can tenderly minister to people and meet them where they're at. I am also able to see how God can directly and uncompromisingly call someone to the carpet on a sin that so entangles and leads others away from Him. God never leaves His people where they are at when it is necessary for them to change. He is always after growth and a returning to Him. He disciplines and restores. He will orchestrate my life so that He can bring about complete restoration and correction in my soul. Mysteriously, God created me in a way that I can come alongside Him in this process. He allows me to enter into the redemptive process He has set before me. I do not have to be afraid and ashamed of how God created me. I can learn from Him and then help others see the same things. God used my daughter to make that point and I will be forever grateful.

What about you? Do you know where God has uniquely gifted you? If not, I would encourage you to figure that out as soon as possible. Two different churches I belonged to throughout the years have used the Uniquely You assessments. You can get an affordable, online version that gives you instant results here: https://www.uniquelyyou.org/catalog/online-profiles/spiritual-gifts. Find books in the Bible that you can read that have themes relating to your gifts and talents.   The important thing is to know how God has created you and to understand that He does not make mistakes.

Joseph was able to know the people under him so well that he could decipher their moods and dispositions. You are to do the same. Be a student of your friends, family, coworkers and even your enemies. Understanding them will help you communicate and serve them better. You also need to understand how the Creator created you. You have a responsibility to understand your gifts and talents and to use them for His glory and furthering His kingdom. Anything short of that is disobedience.

SATAN WANTS YOU TO LIVE YOUR LIFE REACTING TO EVERYTHING. INSTEAD OF TAKING THE TIME TO TRULY UNDERSTAND YOUR FRIENDS, FAMILY AND ENEMIES, HE WANTS YOU TO BE IGNORANT OF HOW THEY PROCESS LIFE AND THEREFORE CONSTANTLY THINK THAT THEY ARE SOMEHOW IN THE WRONG. HE ALSO WANTS YOU TO THINK THAT GOD MADE A MISTAKE WHEN HE CREATED YOU. HE WANTS YOU TO DEVALUE YOUR GIFTS, TALENTS AND ABILITIES.

BUT GOD WANTS YOU TO UNDERSTAND THOSE WITH WHOM HE HAS PLACED YOU IN COMMUNITY. BY UNDERSTANDING THOSE AROUND YOU AND BEING A STUDENT OF THEM, YOU CAN SERVE THEM IN HOLINESS. GOD ALSO WANTS YOU TO KNOW THAT HE CREATED YOU EXACTLY HOW HE MEANT TO CREATE YOU. HE WANTS YOU TO LIVE IN YOUR STRENGTHS AND WITH HIS GUIDANCE, REFINE

YOUR WEAKNESSES. HE WANTS YOU TO KNOW YOU ARE MARKED FOR HIM AND HE CAN ACCOMPLISH GREAT THINGS THROUGH YOU.

Chapter 9

When God Seems to Be Absent

Satan wants to eliminate your hope and cause you to doubt God's presence in your circumstances and doubt His ability to fulfill His promises. BUT GOD wants to prepare you through those circumstances that seem difficult and teach you so that your heart can be revealed to you and to the world.

Genesis 40:23; 41:1a, 9-16, 28b, 32-40

The chief cupbearer, however, did not remember Joseph; he forgot him. When two full years had passed...Then the chief cupbearer said to Pharaoh, "Today I am reminded of my shortcomings. Pharaoh was once angry with his servants, and he imprisoned me and the chief baker in the house of the captain of the guard. Each of us had a dream the same night, and each dream had a meaning of its own. Now a young Hebrew was there with us, a servant of the captain of the guard. We told him our dreams, and he interpreted them for us, giving each man the interpretation of his dream. And things turned out exactly as he interpreted them to us: I was restored to my position, and the other man was impaled." So Pharaoh sent for Joseph, and he was quickly brought from the dungeon. When he had shaved and changed his clothes, he came before Pharaoh. Pharaoh said to Joseph, "I had a dream, and no one can interpret it. But I have heard it said of you that when you hear a dream you can interpret it." "I cannot do it," Joseph replied to Pharaoh, "but God will give Pharaoh the answer he desires...God has shown Pharaoh what he is about to do... The reason the dream was given to Pharaoh in two forms is that the matter has been firmly decided by God, and God will do it soon. And now let Pharaoh look for a discerning and wise man and put him in charge of the land of Egypt. Let Pharaoh appoint commissioners over the land to take a fifth of the harvest of Egypt during the seven years of abundance. They should collect all the food of these good years that are coming and store up the grain under the authority of Pharaoh, to be kept in the cities for food. This food should be held in reserve for the country, to be used during the seven years of famine that will come upon Egypt, so that the country may not be ruined by the famine." The plan seemed good to Pharaoh and to all his officials. So Pharaoh asked them, "Can we find anyone like this man, one in whom is the spirit of God?" Then Pharaoh said to Joseph, "Since God has made all this known to you, there is no one so discerning and wise as you. You shall be in charge of my palace, and all my people are to submit to your orders. Only with respect to the throne will I be greater than you (NIV)."

Everything that had happened in Joseph's life was used to humble him as well as develop his trust in the Lord. If you remember, when Joseph first came to Egypt, he was seventeen years old, or close to it. It was Potiphar who first realized that God was with Joseph. Potiphar had noticed how the Lord had blessed Joseph and decided to put Joseph in charge of his whole household because of that blessing. We are now able to see how Joseph is able to respond to Pharaoh in confidence and faith in the Lord. Joseph rose to power when he was thirty years old. He had been a slave or a prisoner for thirteen years in Egypt. God used every circumstance in his life to prepare him for this moment. Just as God uses every circumstance to prepare you for His calling on your life.

Look at the progression of Joseph's life and you can see God's hand covering it:

1 - He was the favored son of a man who was overseer of his grandfather's flocks. Therefore, he had intimate knowledge on how to be a shepherd over people as well as animals.

2 - Joseph was acquainted with agriculture because his dreams highlighted sheaves of grain. He was at least familiar with planting and harvesting.

3 - Joseph was overseer of the whole household of the captain of the guard. He knew how to delegate, lead, commission, follow through and presumably discipline those under him who did not comply with his orders.

4 - Then he was put in charge of an entire prison. The warden had nothing to fear when Joseph was in charge. Again, his leadership skills were groomed and this time, he was exposed to people who had direct contact with the Pharaoh. Most likely he learned what *not* to do in Pharaoh's presence. He was privy to political information to which he would not have otherwise been exposed.

5 - He was able to have direct, favorable contact with someone who is in the very presence of Pharaoh every single day.

Every single one of these progressions taught and prepared Joseph in unique ways that ultimately garnered him success with Pharaoh. You may not have the privilege of ever seeing the outcome of the circumstances in your life. However, you must approach everything in life as a learning experience. There is something you can learn about yourself, the world, God, or others in each experience. The question is: what are you going to do with the training? How will you respond and react when it counts?

I find myself holding my breath when I read Pharaoh's statement: "I have heard it said of you that when you hear a dream you can interpret it (Genesis 41: 15b NIV)." Do you get the sense that this is a test? Will Joseph acknowledge God or rely on his own abilities? God was testing Joseph to see where his heart was. Was it full of bitterness and bent on revenge back in Dothan? Was it full of pride at being able to interpret correctly the dreams of the cupbearer and the baker? Was it full of doubt because Joseph's own dream hadn't come to fruition yet? God often tests his people to see what is really in their hearts.

Deuteronomy 8:2 says, "Remember how the LORD your God led you all the way in the wilderness these forty years, to humble and test you in order to know what was in your heart, whether or not you would keep his commands (NIV)." Deuteronomy 12:1-3 says, "If a prophet or a dreamer of dreams arises among you and gives you a sign or a wonder, and the sign or wonder that he tells you comes to pass, and if he says, 'Let us go after other gods,' which you have not known, 'and let us serve them,' you shall not listen to the words of that prophet or that dreamer of dreams. For the LORD your God is testing you, to know whether you love the LORD your God with all your heart and with all your soul (ESV)." God cares about the hearts of His people. He longs for a relationship like a father longs for a relationship with his son. He pursues this relationship at a very high cost to Himself. He sends circumstances for training and for learning. He gives His Word for instruction, discipline and revelation of His love. He tests you in order to know where your heart is.

One of my favorite passages is in 2 Chronicles 32. In this chapter we learn about Sennacherib, an Assyrian king who wanted to invade Jerusalem. He sent officers to intimidate the Israelites. They spoke in Hebrew and shouted to all who would listen for Israel not to place their trust in the Lord or in Hezekiah because no other god of any other nation had ever been able to withstand Sennacherib's attacks. Isaiah and Hezekiah cried out to the Lord for salvation and the Lord sent an angel to demolish the Assyrian army. Because of this great victory many gifts and treasures were brought to Jerusalem for the Lord and for King Hezekiah. Around this time, Hezekiah grew deathly ill. He prayed and was miraculously healed but rather than giving humble thanks, the king responded with pride and arrogance, prompting God to become angry and punish Hezekiah and the people of Israel. Realizing his error, Hezekiah repented and spent the rest of his days in peace and prosperity. We pick up the story in verse 27 which states, "Hezekiah was very wealthy and highly honored. He built special treasury buildings for his silver, gold, precious stones, and spices, and for his shields and other valuable items. He also constructed many storehouses for his grain, new wine, and olive oil; and he made many stalls for his cattle and pens for his flocks of sheep and goats. He built many towns and acquired vast flocks and herds, for God had given him great wealth. He blocked up the upper spring of Gihon and brought the water down through a tunnel to the west side of the City of David. And so he succeeded in everything he did. However, when ambassadors arrived from Babylon to ask about the remarkable events that had taken place in the land, God withdrew from Hezekiah in order to test him and to see what was really in his heart (2 Chron. 32:27-31 NLT)."

There are two gems in this passage. One is that it says that Hezekiah "succeeded in everything he did (2 Chron. 32:30 NLT)." Sound familiar? We have just been reading that Joseph succeeded in everything he did as well! Because of God's hand on Hezekiah and God's hand on Joseph they were successful. The question was: to whom were they going to attribute that success?

The second gem, and my favorite image, is in verse 31 where it states, "God withdrew from Hezekiah in order to test him and to see what was really in his heart (NLT)." What a comfort this verse is! When I am praying and I do not know if God is hearing me, or if he cares, I can look to this verse and understand that God purposely withdraws sometimes. God doesn't withdraw in unrighteous anger. God doesn't withdraw in bitterness. God doesn't withdraw because He wants to see me fail. God withdraws because He has prepared me in advance through circumstances, teaching, other people and His Word. He wants to know what is in my heart. God knows exactly what is in my heart. Nothing is hidden from the God of the universe. However, I believe that He withdraws so that it can be made clear to me, where my heart is and if it is fully in tune with His. What a precious gift! While God is always with me, He will, at the right time, withdraw to reveal to me where my heart is in relationship to Him. We don't have to despair when we don't sense God's presence. We do not need to think that He has left us in anger, frustration or hatred. He could just be revealing your heart. What a gracious God we serve!

We see how Joseph passed the test in two ways: First, He denied being able to accomplish anything on his own, but gave honor to God and second, He still trusted God's revelation to him. Joseph was honest with the Pharaoh. He told Pharaoh that it was not he but rather God who could interpret the dreams. Joseph was also able to use his expertise that he had gained from all of the experiences in his past. God used everything from the dreams of a child all the way through to the captivity of an adult. Joseph was able to answer in humility with the right understanding of who God is and who Joseph was. He was able to answer in truth about what God was going to accomplish, what God was going to allow to happen and how Pharaoh needed to act to align himself with God's revelation.

Joseph also references the fact that two dreams meant that "the matter ha[d] been firmly decided by God, and God [would] do it soon. (Genesis 41:32 NIV)." Was Joseph preaching to his own heart? In that moment, I wonder if his words got caught in his throat. I imagine he got choked up with a little bit of sadness, or longing for his dreams to also come true. Of course it is supposition, but even if there was a little twinge of self-pity, it did not waver Joseph's faith. He was confident in who God is and how He fulfills His promises, a fact that Joseph had come to understand through the many strange events of his life.

In God's sovereignty, Joseph was elevated to second in command! I am convinced none of this would have happened if Joseph had not gone through all of the experiences in his past. God prepared him and then tested him to see where his heart was.

SATAN WANTS YOU TO THINK THAT GOD HAS LEFT YOU. YOU ARE ON YOUR OWN AND YOU NEED TO FEND FOR YOURSELF. EVERY SITUATION IS WHAT IT IS AND THERE IS NO HIGHER PURPOSE, SO SUFFERING IS JUST SUFFERING AND PAIN IS JUST PAIN BECAUSE A GOOD GOD WOULD NOT ALLOW PAIN AND SUFFERING. THERE IS NO HOPE.

BUT GOD WANTS YOU TO KNOW THAT HE HAS ORDAINED EVERYTHING IN YOUR LIFE AND WILL USE IT TO FURTHER HIS ULTIMATE PURPOSE. YOU CAN LEARN FROM ALL YOUR EXPERIENCES

AND SEE GOD'S GOODNESS. GOD IS ALWAYS WITH YOU, EVEN WHEN IT SEEMS LIKE HE IS ABSENT. HE WILL OFTEN PRESENT YOU WITH TESTS TO REVEAL WHERE YOUR HEART IS ALIGNED.

Chapter 10
Living the Lies

Satan wants you to continue living your life grounded in the lies you
believe because of the patterns of your past.
BUT GOD wants you know that He can redeem your past and cause you to
throw off the lies and start living in the light of His truth and instead of
staying stagnant and emotionally impotent, you can actually be fruitful.

Genesis 41:50-52; 49:22-26

**During this time, before the first of the famine years, two sons
were born to Joseph and his wife, Asenath, the daughter of
Potiphera, the priest of On. Joseph named his older son
Manasseh, for he said, "God has made me forget all my troubles
and everyone in my father's family." Joseph named his second son
Ephraim, for he said, "God has made me fruitful in this land of my
grief..."**
[Israel's blessing over Joseph just before he died.]

**Joseph is a fruitful vine,
a fruitful vine near a spring,
whose branches climb over a wall.**

**With bitterness archers attacked him;
they shot at him with hostility.**

**But his bow remained steady,
his strong arms stayed limber,**

**because of the hand of the Mighty One of Jacob,
because of the Shepherd, the Rock of Israel,**

because of your father's God, who helps you,

because of the Almighty, who blesses you

with blessings of the skies above,
blessings of the deep springs below,
blessings of the breast and womb.

Your father's blessings are greater
than the blessings of the ancient mountains,
than the bounty of the age-old hills.

Let all these rest on the head of Joseph,
on the brow of the prince among his brothers (NIV).

I absolutely love how God never leaves us alone. He is constantly working on us, in us and through us. Joseph has just gathered all the food from the seven years of bumper crops. He is overseer and second in command. However, in these verses where we see the names of his children, we are given a glimpse of his heart. Joseph is still wrestling with the feelings of abandonment and betrayal. Even after his success, everywhere he went for that matter, a piece of him still ached and was broken. With the birth of his first son Manasseh, he was able to come to a place where he no longer remembered the troubles that came to him as a child. He was able to move forward from his past. He was able to see God's goodness and God's presence. With the birth of his second son Ephraim, we see how he acknowledges that God has made him fruitful and successful. It appears that he had been focusing on Egypt as the land of his grief. The land where everything was taken away from him and he was reduced to nothing. He is finally able to see how God has made him successful and blessed him wherever he went whether it was Potiphar's house, the prison, or the palace.

Childhood pain resulting from injustices at the hands of your parents or at the hands of your so-called friends can last a lifetime. It takes years to be able to see God's hand in circumstances and to be able to rise above them and come out on the other side of your grief. Even if you did not experience childhood trauma, high school alone is enough to alter your perception of yourself and the world around you for years to come. Based on your past there are lies that you will believe about yourself for a very long time. An excellent book to help in the process of erasing old messages written on your heart and walking in a new light is the book, "Rewriting Your Emotional Script," by Becky Harling. In this book, she walks you through the Beatitudes and shows you how to embrace new attitudes and erase the old messages in your mind and heart. She quotes one of her friends on page 53 and says, "As we go through the process of mourning, we grieve our losses and draw near to God. He is able to heal our wounds in a way that create softness in our hearts, making us ready for change in the right direction. Once we have gone through this process, we know that God will always grow and transform us through our trials and sufferings. This blesses us."

Harling encourages you to create a "timeline of your life (27)." Think about the major events in your life and what those events taught you.
- Did they teach you that you need to be perfect?
- Did they teach you that you would never be believed?
- Did they teach you that crying is not allowed?
- Did they teach you that you can't trust anybody?
- Did they teach you that you need to be in control emotionally, physically and spatially? What lies are you believing? **Check out the Joseph Study Guide to help you dig deeper into how these events shaped your thinking.**

When you have experienced pain in your past, you seek to control the world around you. Harling writes on pages 74-75, "...We begin to rely on our own abilities to reestablish order in our chaotic world. We tried to build security and structure with our own hands rather than relying on God provided these things for us. As a result, destructive patterns of control show up in the most unexpected ways and at the most inopportune times. What are some of these patterns? Worry or anxiety, manipulation, nagging, eating issues, bossiness, rigidity, black and white thinking, difficulty delegating, workaholic patterns, tension, perfectionism" to name a few. She encourages readers to "rewrite the lies [that they grew] up believing and replace them with God's life-giving truth. Rather than focusing on what [bullies, insensitive relatives, angry bosses, abusive parents or backstabbing friends] taught you about God's character...meditate on what the Bible say[s] about" who God is (Harling 86). Make a list of His attributes and "then next to each, write down why this trait provides a good reason for you to trust him. Then thank him for each quality. Write out a prayer of praise that is based on your list. (Harling 87)." This book is utterly invaluable when it comes to healing from past hurts.

It appears that Joseph and God had to walk through something similar. God had to take Joseph from a place of grief, sorrow, betrayal and despair and bring him to a point of acknowledging God's protection, provision and providence. The ultimate goal is to realize the fruit that has come from your life. You can be fruitful despite the pain of your past. You can prosper and be successful physically as well as emotionally.

SATAN WANTS YOU TO LIVE YOUR FUTURE WITHOUT VICTORY OVER YOUR PAST. HE WANTS YOU TO WALLOW IN SHAME, FEAR, GUILT AND DESPAIR. HE WANTS YOU TO THINK THAT YOU WILL NEVER BE ABLE TO SHAKE THE MEMORIES, OR HAVE MASTERY OVER YOUR EMOTIONS. HE ONLY WANTS YOU TO REMEMBER THE PAIN AND THE HARD CIRCUMSTANCES THAT HAVE DAMAGED YOU WHETHER THAT BE PHYSICAL AND EMOTIONAL TRAUMA OR DEEP SORROW AND HURT FEELINGS. HE WANTS YOU TO CONTINUE TO LIVE THE LIES.

BUT GOD WANTS YOU TO KNOW HE CAN MAKE SOMETHING FRUITFUL AND BEAUTIFUL OUT OF THE ASHES OF YOUR PAST. HE CAN CAUSE YOU TO GROW AND MATURE AND CHANGE INTO A STRONG WARRIOR OF GOD. HE LONGS FOR YOU TO REALIZE THAT THE LIES OF YOUR PAST DO NOT DEFINE WHO YOU ARE IN CHRIST.

Chapter 11

When Dreams Take a While to Materialize

Satan wants you to believe that God is a liar because you are living with dreams unrealized.
BUT GOD wants you to experience the lessons learned in the waiting period to prepare you for what He has in store.

Genesis 42:8-9a, 23-24

Although Joseph recognized his brothers, they didn't recognize him. And he remembered the dreams he'd had about them many years before...Of course, they didn't know that Joseph understood them, for he had been speaking to them through an interpreter. Now he turned away from them and began to weep. When he regained his composure, he spoke to them again. Then he chose Simeon from among them and had him tied up right before their eyes (NLT)."

God prepared Joseph to face his enemies. I think he was crying for two reasons. One is the obvious, that it was raw and painful to see his brothers. We will talk about the reason he was crying in the next chapter. Secondly, he was suddenly hit with the answer to his dreams of his youth. He saw how far he had come on his journey of forgiveness and had witnessed God's hand in it all. He was finally blessed to see God's plan and it was overwhelming and wonderful.

Joseph was able to see how God had fulfilled his calling. The Scriptures say, "And he remembered the dreams he'd had about them many years before (Genesis 42:9a NLT)." He knew that this was the moment. He was fulfilling his calling that God had issued long ago. It took betrayal, slavery, imprisonment and exultation to get him there. Imagine the emotions that would bring out in a person. To finally see your life flash before your eyes. You see how God orchestrated it all. To remember your youth when you thought things would turn out one way, to see how they actually turned out and to marvel at how God is so intimately involved in your life. He holds the universe in His hands, yet He intricately coordinates every aspect of your life! Every tiny detail. He is in control and nothing is impossible for Him. How outstanding to be able to witness His sovereignty. The weight and impact of that revelation is enough to bring anyone to their knees!

Have you ever waited a long time for dreams to be realized? Maybe you have waited and waited for a child and you finally got the call from the adoption agency that the paperwork is ready. Perhaps you have finally gotten your degree. Have you recently paid off your debt and now you are experiencing financial freedom for the first time? Are you finally pain free?

One of the most beautiful women I know received Christ after she was married. Naturally, as any woman would, she wanted her husband to also come to Jesus. In her excitement of being newly saved, she tried in vain to convert her husband. Season after season, year after year, decade after decade she would attempt to plant seeds. Tracks were given and thrown away. Conversations were started but quickly shut down. She finally gave him up to her Lord and Savior and never ceased praying for him.

Her children were brought up in the church and also grew to love the Lord and both serve Him with all their hearts today. Together as a family, they have prayed for upwards of 30 years for the salvation of their father and husband. Our church has continually prayed for him as well. I have been praying for him for as long as I can remember. This dear woman was a Sunday School teacher of mine and she really had a large impact on me. I saw her serve our church and her husband with selflessness, gratitude and joy. My heart would ache for her as I grew up, went to college, married and started a family of my own. I could not imagine raising children and struggling through life with a husband who did not share the same faith as me. That would devastate me; therefore, she and her husband were often on my heart.

Our church held a 90th birthday party for my mother. I noticed this woman's husband was there but I thought he was there to celebrate my mother's birthday. I told my mother that it was nice to see him in church and she informed me that he had, at ninety-two years of age accepted Christ! He had been attending church, reading his Bible and listening to sermons at home! Decades of praying and dreaming what it would be like to be married to a believing husband was finally realized for this faithful woman! Can you imagine her joy? Her gratitude? Her astonishment? I imagine the flood of emotions that went through her when she heard that he had accepted Christ was similar to the deluge that washed over Joseph upon encountering his siblings as they bowed down to him.

SATAN WANTS YOU TO GIVE UP ON GOD. HE WANTS YOU TO QUESTION WHAT GOD HAS LAID ON YOUR HEART. HE WANTS YOU TO SCRAP YOUR DREAMS AT THE EARLIEST OBSTACLE. HE WANTS YOU TO FORGET WHAT LIT THE FIRE IN THE FIRST PLACE.

BUT GOD WANTS YOU TO PERSEVERE REGARDLESS OF TIMING. EVERYTHING IS ON HIS PERFECT SCHEDULE AND HE WANTS YOU TO SUBMIT YOUR DREAMS AND YOUR TIMETABLE TO HIM. HE IS TRUSTWORTHY AND KNOWS WHAT IS BEST FOR YOU.

Chapter 12
The Hard Road of Forgiveness

Satan wants you to be so consumed by bitterness and resentment that
your only focus is destruction and revenge.
BUT GOD wants you to understand true forgiveness by learning what
your enemy needs and then providing that for that person which could
mean physical, emotional or spiritual aid and/or discipline.

Genesis 50:15-21

**When Joseph's brothers saw that their father was dead, they said,
"What if Joseph holds a grudge against us and pays us back for all
the wrongs we did to him?" So they sent word to Joseph, saying,
"Your father left these instructions before he died: 'This is what you
are to say to Joseph: I ask you to forgive your brothers the sins and
the wrongs they committed in treating you so badly.' Now please
forgive the sins of the servants of the God of your father." When their
message came to him, Joseph wept. His brothers then came and
threw themselves down before him. "We are your slaves," they
said. But Joseph said to them, "Don't be afraid. Am I in the place of
God? You intended to harm me, but God intended it for good to
accomplish what is now being done, the saving of many lives. So
then, don't be afraid. I will provide for you and your children." And
he reassured them and spoke kindly to them (NIV)**

There was much to forgive: familial verbal and physical abuse, the
hardships encountered at the hands of slave drivers, false accusations
and wrongful imprisonment. Bitterness could have easily taken root
in Joseph's heart. From a human standpoint, we would not have
blamed him if he let resentment and anger grow deep within
him. But God was with Joseph. God showed him kindness. He
allowed Joseph to be successful and prosper and find favor under his
masters. He was allowed freedoms within his slavery and

imprisonment. Joseph realized that a good and loving God allowed those circumstances to come to pass as well as really try to understand and know intimately, who he needed to forgive.

When Joseph was accused by Potiphar's wife, he could have been executed for attempted rape of the wife of the head of the royal guard. The fact that Joseph was sent to the prison where the prisoners of the Pharaoh were sent is another amazing piece of God's puzzle.   It is here in the prison where Joseph must have learned a lesson in forgiveness. He was falsely accused. He was upright and most likely other slaves knew he was innocent. Perhaps even Potiphar knew he was innocent, but his hands were tied because of his wife's public outcry. That could be the reason Joseph was sent to prison instead of execution. God had provided a way out of the temptation to sleep with Potiphar's wife. It was there where God tinkered with Joseph's heart and helped him forgive the sins of his past.

God brought Joseph to a place of forgiveness. He can bring you there too. God worked on Joseph in the dark days. Joseph first had to recognize and see God's providence in the situation. He had to acknowledge that God had allowed everything that happened to him. That is tough to swallow. A God in whom you should place your trust allowed negative things to impact you. You have a choice: will you believe God is good and trust His plan or will you turn your back on your Creator? Joseph faced this choice as well. Was he going to recognize that God caused him to prosper and He was with him every step of the way? I believe that his father's "faith testimony" and recognizing God's provision of his success helped to recognize God's sovereignty.   God had created and molded Joseph to be the man he was in the end. The man who wept over his brothers' fear. The man who could say that they meant evil to befall him, but God meant it all to save the lives of countless others.

Joseph also had to understand exactly what his enemies (his brothers) needed to live and flourish. When his brothers returned, He was able to give them what they needed. He was able to provide for them physically (grain), emotionally (forgiveness) and spiritually (acknowledging God's hand in it all).

Romans 12:14-21 says, "Bless those who persecute you; bless and do not curse. Rejoice with those who rejoice; mourn with those who mourn. Live in harmony with one another. Do not be proud, but be willing to associate with people of low position. Do not be conceited. Do not repay anyone evil for evil. Be careful to do what is right in the eyes of everybody. If it is possible, as far as it depends on you, live at peace with everyone. Do not take revenge, my friends, but leave room for God's wrath, for it is written: 'It is mine to avenge; I will repay,' says the Lord. On the contrary: 'If your enemy is hungry, feed him; if he is thirsty, give him something to drink. In doing this, you will heap burning coals on his head.' Do not be overcome by evil, but overcome evil with good (NIV)." A friend of mine said to think about in what way your enemy is hungry and thirsty. What might the root of the animosity between you be? I thought this was a profound statement. I had never thought about looking at the verses: "If your enemy is hungry, feed him; if he is thirsty, give him something to drink," and thinking beyond their physical needs (Romans 12:20 NIV). I thought, "If I see my enemy with a flat tire on the side of the road, I should stop and offer assistance." Think about it: perhaps they need love, attention, wisdom or even boundaries. Maybe they need someone to mourn with them or laugh with them. Give them what they stand in need of. If it is tough love, then so be it. Love them "toughly." If the natural consequence is to sever ties for a while, then let go of the ties and let the consequences be the teachers. If it is prayer because their husband has been caught in an affair, then pray for them. If they constantly overstep their boundaries and try to manipulate your every move, perhaps setting up a fence or hedge is in order. You do what needs to be done for them.

In this way, "you will heap burning coals on his head (Romans 12:21 NIV)." There are differing views on what this phrase signifies. I have heard it said before that heaping burning coals on someone's head was not a negative act. Back then, people used fire to warm their houses as well as cook. If their embers went out, it would take a long time for the wood to turn to coals for food preparation. If an enemy neighbor would come to you and ask for some coals, you would not give him one coal because that would not be helpful. You would heap a bunch of burning coals on the pan or bowl in which he carries the coals (that he also carries on his head). You would be helping him provide life and survival for his family.

In other words, provide for your enemy what he/she is lacking that is causing spiritual death. Quench their thirst and calm their hunger with what they truly need - maybe not what they want, but what they actually need. In so doing, you will move them from a place of deadness (no coals to sustain life) to a place of life, warmth and vibrancy.

SATAN WANTS YOU PREOCCUPIED WITH BITTERNESS. HE WANTS FORGIVENESS TO BE THE FARTHEST THING FROM YOUR MIND. HE WANTS YOU TO WALLOW IN THE ABUSE, HURT AND PAIN OF THE PAST SO THAT YOU CAN NEVER MOVE FORWARD. IF YOU KEEP SPINNING YOUR WHEELS, YOU WILL NEVER BE ABLE TO GET OUT OF THE DITCH AND ON THE PATH OF RIGHTEOUSNESS.

BUT GOD WANTS YOU TO PROVIDE LIFE TO THOSE WHOM YOU NEED TO FORGIVE. YOU ARE TO SEEK OUT WHAT YOUR ENEMY NEEDS AND WILLINGLY GIVE TO THAT PERSON. GOD CAN WORK A MIRACLE IN YOUR SOUL AND PROTECT AND RESTORE YOUR JOY. HE WILL HELP YOU ON THE PATH OF FORGIVENESS.

STOP! BEFORE YOU GO ANY FURTHER, ACCESS THE **FREE**, DOWNLOADABLE *Study Guide* HERE:

http://visitor.r20.constantcontact.com/d.jsp?llr=qyarwexab&p=oi&m=1124 365533968&sit=z7tlokqkb&f=8298aefb-3e02-419e-b440-610589fe255a

Acknowledgements

Words cannot express the thankfulness that flows from my heart to all of the people who helped make this bucket list item possible. My husband and children – thank you for putting up with all of the laundry piles and general lack of household order while this was coming together. Your graciousness has taught me a lot. Though, I'll be glad to get my favorite workout pants back from the black hole that is the hamper!

Eryn Sluiter, my VA, thank you so much for tackling other projects so I could focus on this. That was an enormous help! Your encouragement and belief in me is a lifeline. Your willingness to think big gives me permission to dream the impossible.

My editors – Amy, Stacey, Jennifer, Sarah, Brenda, Donna and gingermaneditor (from Fiverr.com). This manuscript would NOT be half as legible if it were not for you! Your support and the time you took to read the chapters and give me feedback is GREATLY appreciated.

My friends who always seem to say what I need to hear at just the right moment. You know who you are because I've told you countless times that I needed to hear what you've said. You span the country from California to Missouri to Michigan to Virginia and Connecticut. I am so blessed.

Finally, as the Alpha and Omega, the Author and Finisher of my faith, my LORD and Savior, Jesus Christ. Why you allow me to enter into Your will is beyond me. My life is yours.

Don't miss out on the experience!

Access your FREE Study Guide TODAY!

http://visitor.r20.constantcontact.com/d.jsp?llr=qyarwexab&p=oi&m
=1124365533968&sit=z7tlokqkb&f=8298aefb-3e02-419e-b440-
610589fe255a

Additional Resources

CHAPTER 1
Cunningham, Ted. <u>Trophy Child: Saving Parents from Performance, Preparing Children for Something Greater than Themselves</u>. (Colorado Springs, CO: David C Cook, 2012), 22-23; 26-27.

CHAPTER 2
Daly, Jim. "Dinner: Nourish Your Family ... As a Family." *Focus on the Family*. Focus on the Family, 11 June 2012. Web. 03 Apr. 2016.

CHAPTER 4
"Ancient Cisterns - Background Bible Study (Bible History Online)." *Ancient Cisterns - Background Bible Study* (Bible History Online). Rusty Russell, n.d. Web. 03 Apr. 2016.

CHAPTER 8
Koch, Dr. Kathy. "8 Great Smarts." Interview by Dr. Gary Chapman, Chris Fabry, and Andrea Fabry. *Building Relationships*. Moody Bible Radio. 89.3, Zeeland, MI, 02 Apr. 2016. Radio.

Tobias, Cynthia Ulrich. *Every Child Can Succeed: Making the Most of Your Child's Learning Style*. (Colorado Springs, CO: Focus on the Family Pub.), 1996. Print.

Chapman, Gary D. *The Five Love Languages: How to Express Heartfelt Commitment to Your Mate*. (Chicago: Northfield Pub., 1995). Print.

Carbonell, Dr. Mels. "Spiritual Gifts | Uniquely You." *Spiritual Gifts | Uniquely You*. Dr, n.d. Web. 03 Apr. 2016. <https://www.uniquelyyou.org/catalog/online-profiles/spiritual-gifts>.

CHAPTER 10
Harling, Becky. *Rewriting Your Emotional Script: Erase Old Messages, Embrace New Attitudes*. (Colorado Springs, CO: NavPress, 2008), 27; 53; 74-75; 86-87.